# Brill W[illegible]alks

## [illegible]ne Peak

## Book Three



Circular walks in and around
Castleton and Edale
The Reservoirs
Miller's Dale
Chatsworth and Baslow

Photographs: Bob Brill
Tales: Freda Bowman
Maps: Roger Penney

Freda Bowman

Bob Brill

# Introduction

We have been delighted that **'Brill Walks'** books one and two have proved to be such a success. The book sales have exceeded all expectations and many of our readers have urged us to produce this third volume.

The format of the other two books has been so popular that we have kept to it in this one. Again, the book consists of twelve thoroughly researched walks, and includes some of our favourites, in the most spectacular and dramatic areas of the Peak District. Each walk has much to offer in beauty, variety and points of interest, and again we feel confident that the first one you attempt will encourage you to walk all the others.

As always, we have taken immense care to make the route instructions clear and totally confusion free, so that although simple maps are provided, these are intended only as general indicators of the point you have reached on the route. Nor is it assumed that you will carry an Ordnance Survey map, although starting point grid references are given.

The walks have all been carefully checked by friends and family to ensure there are no areas of uncertainty.

However, it is important to remember that the countryside is a living environment, so changes can occur. A stile, for example, may be replaced with a gate, etc. We have tried to minimise the possible effects of changes by the form of instructions we use and the choice of waymarks to guide you.

Particular points of interest are highlighted on each walk and we hope these will add to your enjoyment. It's the next best thing to having a local guide with you!

All these walks are circular. They vary in length and terrain and the general summary before each one will help you to make your choice.

In the beautiful Derbyshire countryside it is very difficult to avoid a few hills, and we are assuming our walkers are of normal health and fitness. It's worth a mention that our walks have been enjoyed by people of all ages.

Because many surfaces are uneven and certain areas can sometimes be muddy, lightweight walking boots are recommended for all our walks.

For all of the four areas in which the walks are located, there is a short story. Each is set in an interesting time of that place's history. The general details of the historical settings are researched and accurate. Four very different people, with contrasting lives, tell their own stories. Many people have commented that their experience of walking these areas has been enhanced by reading these tales.

We have had great fun both walking and writing our third book and our pleasure has been increased by the knowledge that so many others will share this enjoyment with us.

# Contents

## Castleton and Edale Area



## Litton and the Dales



## The Reservoirs



## Chatsworth and Baslow Area

# The Castleton and Edale Walks

*Edale Valley from Mam Tor*

*Castleton*

*Visitor Centre, Castleton*

*Peak Cavern*

# The Deathbed Tale

God knows, it's something we all have to face in the end, but that man faced it far worse than most. No words I said gave the slightest comfort to him, nothing I did seem to ease his pain - neither sips of brandy, nor a damp rag to his forehead, nor any rearrangement of the soiled covers on his unkempt bed.

I've been there for the last hours of more than I could now count, and to most I can bring a sense of calm, a soothing touch from my wrinkled hands, a feeling of coolness to overheated flesh. "Fetch old Kate," they say in this village, as the end draws close, and especially if that end's not looking like being a peaceful one.

But of course they fetch old Kate at the beginning of things, as well, and even more urgently. There's precious few young souls in Castleton not helped into the world by me. Not unless a woman's caught out by the speed of things, and even then I'm brought to the home straight after. It's me who cuts the cord, me who washes the blood from the two of them. They all know I don't lose very many, neither babes nor mothers. God has given me a good pair of hands and a healing touch. Even when they're not lying right, I can generally ease them out. Not every one of course, but then, God never willed that all those born should live. There are the ones destined to die. But I do my best with the gifts he has given me.

Not that I've always been able to devote myself to it, not as a young woman. When you're born into this place, into a Castleton family of rope-makers going back many generations, then that's what's naturally expected of you. And that's what I used to be doing - for years on end - hating every minute spent in the gaping mouth of that huge cavern. Though you'd have to say 'mouth' is the wrong word for a place known as the Devil's Arse! Better bred folks - usually those who haven't laboured there - give it the name of Peak Cavern. That's where most of our village's rope walks are, and that's where I spent my waking hours with the rest of them, walking back and forth, back and forth - God knows how many miles a day. The fibres would be tied loosely around our waists, and we'd be twisting and plaiting them into cord as we stepped slowly backwards from the spinning wheels. Then forward once more towards the wheels, to start the whole process again, and again and yet again. The cord would thicken very slightly with each backward journey. Gloomy and dank in there, of course, but ample space for a good number of families to ply their trade, each one laying claim to its special terrace, carved out on the cavern floor. Some even lived inside the place, and still do! A row of small houses has been built in there, a one-roomed inn as well, all of them crouching under that overpowering greyness of the cave's great roof. Smoke from their chimneys has made great black patches on the rock ceiling above. As you can imagine, the atmosphere within is one of acrid damp.

No, it was never the place for me, and I shudder at the memory. But others in there would not change their lives or their means of making a living. They love the chatter, the gossip, the crude laughter, all those clanging, echoing sounds, and they enjoy the looks of wonder on the faces of travellers, who can scarcely believe that life can be lived and work done in such a place, and with such good spirits.

I did not make my escape, of course, for many years. Not until I had lost my youth, not until I had helped very many in the village to be born, to bear illness, or to face death. For it was me, over the years, folk began naturally to turn to. Who else was there? None with a touch like mine. And finally there was no time for the making of ropes and cords. It was best left to those who felt a pride in that trade. My own hands were released for the real skill that lay in them.

But I have wandered from my subject - the dying, the very difficult dying, of James Ashton, once a worker in the Odin Mine, now lying before me in a state of pain and desperation. Perhaps lead poisoning? It carries off many a miner, drink hard as they might. I am not a believer that ale can protect from such a curse of a disease, though most men give it an ample enough try. But James Ashton's suffering seemed to me to be beyond his physical plight. There was an agony playing out in his mind, the like of which I had not experienced in any before. I sensed it plainly, as I sensed his urge to speak, and of course there was but me for him to speak with. Few others, for many years, had chosen to enter the boundaries of that man's life, and none had entered far.

I was forced to touch his cheek with my own in order to catch his words. No other would have done so - not for this taciturn, surly man, without a vestige of human warmth. On his deathbed, Ashton's face was contorted and ugly - as many are - and his body evil-smelling. These are not difficulties for me. I am there for all, I do not allow myself to be repelled.

"Beaut..i…ful"…….. I finally made out that long word, which I knew made no reference to me. No man has ever called me beautiful. Not even in those far gone days, when I would not infrequently be followed home by some lusting youth, clearly hoping that since I was so very plain, I would welcome the advances of any man. Even one who required but a brief coupling in the dark recesses of a nearby barn.

James Ashton turned his head towards me, the movement sending a clear ripple of pain across his face. His dry lips struggled to move once again….. "Killed them……. both of them…….. all of us…… killed them." A few moments then, to draw in a long, final, rasping breath….. "Hacked them….. axes….. both of them."

There were no more words beyond these. As minutes passed, and the rattle of his chest ceased, I knew death was present, and muttered a simple prayer for the journey of his soul. Whether God listened, I do not know. That I had been the hearer of a final confession, there was no doubt.

I am not a priest, I am bound by no laws of secrecy. I instantly knew in my heart of what crime James Ashton spoke, it was surely now my duty to make that known to others. If nothing else, the living kin of that poor young couple could know the truth of their fate.

About ten years ago, it was, their bodies were found. That's if you can call two piles of shattered bones by the name of bodies. Lying at the bottom of a mine in Winnats Pass, and very likely to have been thrown down there, it was thought. That's what the miners believed, the ones who found them, while they were busy sinking an engine pit. The two corpses, or what remained of them, were pulled up and buried in the churchyard, a few belated prayers said briefly over them. And then the numbers two and two were put together, and a four came up loud and clear, because about ten years prior to that event - 1758, it was, the year stays with me - a young man and woman had arrived in the village on horseback, and taken a meal in a Castleton inn. Noticed by a good number of people, and not least by the landlord. At the time, he was busy trying to throw out a group of drunken miners - four of them, so he recalled - and having finally done so, he put this couple in the inn's parlour, where they could have a bit of comfort and quiet. He remembered the young lady as being very lovely-looking indeed. And as a healthy and not too old a man himself at the time - well - it's not a thing he would be unaware of, obviously not. There are girls in this village with coarsely attractive faces, but rarely do we see a more delicate form of beauty. Harsh weather, long hours of labour, damp homes without comfort - these take an early and a heavy toll. So this handsome young woman, with soft skin, clean, lush hair and a gentle voice must have stood out for him like a flower among a bed of weeds. Any man would take notice of her, drink her in, look at her with some desire. And not forget her either, for such visitors are rare. I doubt he paid much attention to her companion, although, when later pressed to recall, he suggested that this was no ordinary working man, could not have been confused with the loud, abrasive miners. The pair of them, he said, had an air of money about them. And not only in their appearance, but in the actual leather purses they could be seen holding, and discussing.

But she had confided to him, so this innkeeper claimed - as he had served them in the parlour and enquired about their journey - that they were making their way to a church in the village of Peak Forest. The Church of Charles, King and Martyr. They had been travelling for some days, she said, and even mentioned stopping at an inn in Stoney Middleton, their horses having been, at that point, in dire need of food and rest. But now they were anxious to complete their journey, without further delay. At this point, the landlord assumed, quite naturally, that they must be runways. The Church of Peak Forest is well known for attracting couples from many miles around, whose family (or more precisely, the father of such a family) refuses consent to their marriage. For the minister of King Charles's church is bound by none of the usual clerical duties of announcing banns, calling witnesses, ensuring that all is regular and proper. I am unable now to recall the reason for this, but in my memory it has always been so. Many a rich and important family would dearly love to see it changed! For that minister's door can be knocked upon at any time of day, indeed he can be awoken in the night at any hour, and a simple wedding ceremony can take place there and then - provided appropriate payment is made. Almost certainly, like others before them, these two were seeking such a secretive means of union.

They left the inn a couple of hours later, the landlord no doubt reluctant to release the enthralling sight of her, feeling, perhaps, an instinctive envy of her companion, who mounted the larger of their barely rested horses. An enticingly pleasant episode, in his hard-working and predictable life.

Within days, it became known that no such young couple had ever reached the Church of King Charles. Members of two families - an important, even aristocratic one, in her case - were making inquiries in this village, as in others. Rumours began rumbling through Castleton. The minister of Peak Forest Church found himself questioned (not, I'm quite sure, a new experience for him), and eventually the trail led to our own innkeeper. But he could speak only of the young people's visit, of their departure, of their stated destination. Desire and envy - and he was a man known to be capable of both, as I have suggested - had in fact been given no free rein. Of that I, and most others, felt sure.

Perhaps Allan and Clara - we now learned their names, though surnames were never to be known - had met death by wandering from the rough and ill-marked path and falling down some open mineshaft. A common enough fate, far from unusual in these parts. Especially easy when a traveller is weary and unalert. But the two horses had been found within hours, wandering alone and bathed in heavy sweats, difficult to calm. They still wore saddles and bridles but the large saddlebags were empty - not a single item lay within them. Suspicions of robbery, of violent death, quickly took hold. But the finger of accusation could not be pointed at any man.

But now I knew. Now I knew who had killed those two, twenty years ago, armed with a pickaxe and consumed by greed. And perhaps driven by lust, too. How can we ever know? But this man had not killed alone, of course. James Ashton, a particularly foul-mouthed and brutish man - but a strong and hard-working miner in his day - was a regular drinker, and a regular drunkard, at the very inn I have spoken of. Often along with a few companions, with whom he argued incessantly and occasionally challenged into fighting. These were the men unceremoniously pushed out of the inn door, as the landlord later clearly recalled, after which he was able to entertain Clara and her companion in greater comfort. The men were seen to stumble across the street towards the shabby cottage of another of their group, their shouts loud and uncouth. But not, it was now plain, before the attractive young couple, in their smart riding-clothes, had been noted.

How easy to lurk nearby, awaiting their departure. How pleasing to note them heading out towards the rugged and desolate Winnats Pass. What a satisfying way to assuage drunken anger and sour resentment.

Yes, there had been thoughts, dark thoughts, concerning these men in the village. It had always been a mystery how James Ashton managed to buy himself a bunch of good quality horses, not so very long after that couple's disappearance. Strange for the daughter of one of his drinking companions to appear in church wearing a well cut silk dress, vastly beyond her family's means or even their imagination. But no-one could know, and these were not men to antagonise, let alone accuse, lightly. Life can be dangerous in a village. So no-one spoke loudly, no accusers or witnesses came forward, and no make-shift gallows were ordered to be constructed. The nooses - which almost certainly would have been made from our own village's rope - were escaped.

James Ashton was the last of them. He had outlived his companions by some years and, as I look back, I realise that all those men died strangely. John Bradshaw was killed by a falling rock, not far, in fact, from the shaft into which those poor hacked up bodies were dropped. Nicholas Cock also died near that place, missing his foothold and falling from a precipice, his head dashed open on the rock-strewn ground. And the other two? Thomas Hall and Francis Butler? Hall hanged himself in his own house. He had spoken to no-one for weeks, and his body was not found for many days. Francis Butler, always an unstable character, became madder as the years went by. Towards his end, no person could reach him, and no one tried to. Madness is much feared, it is often seen as the work of the devil. In his final weeks, he would not tolerate even me at his bedside. He shrieked out to be left alone, and this I felt I had no choice but to do.

Of them all, only James Ashton has died in my presence. Only he has spoken of guilt. May God have mercy on him.

I am an old and frail woman - not far from death myself, I strongly sense. Seventy-eight years - more aged than any other soul in this village. I will tend to them all while there is still strength in me, but some other, a younger woman, must soon take on the heavy mantle of care for birth and illness and death.

The simple homes of Castleton huddle together, now as then, in their narrow valley. Perched on a thin crust of earth above vast caverns and mines, surrounded by crags and wilderness. Should you choose to visit the place, you will no doubt find it to be charming and welcoming - a sweet village of unique attractiveness. It is such, of course, without a doubt. But evil has been done here, as everywhere. The beauty of a place offers no protection against it.

## Historical Note

Even today, the dramatic Winnats Pass can seem, especially in winter, bleak and desolate. In the mid-18th century, when the events of this tale took place, it would have been lonelier and no doubt appeared even more menacing.

The murder of travellers - probably not, at the time, an extraordinary event in itself - turned out to be memorable in the case of Allan and Clara. Almost certainly it was the wild landscape in which the brutal killing took place, and the likely romantic reason for the journey, which gave these two people their place in local history.

The words of this tale are spoken by a fictional character, the old nurse. The people she speaks of, however, were real and all the events and circumstances she mentions are believed to be true.

For hundreds of years, Castleton was known for its rope making, much of which took place in the huge and gloomy entrance to Peak Cavern. Whole families were involved, and skills passed down through the generations. Rope walks were constructed along terraces, cut into the cavern floor. Remains of this industry can still be viewed in the Peak Cavern.

# Walk 1

## Castleton
## Cave Dale
## Winnats Pass

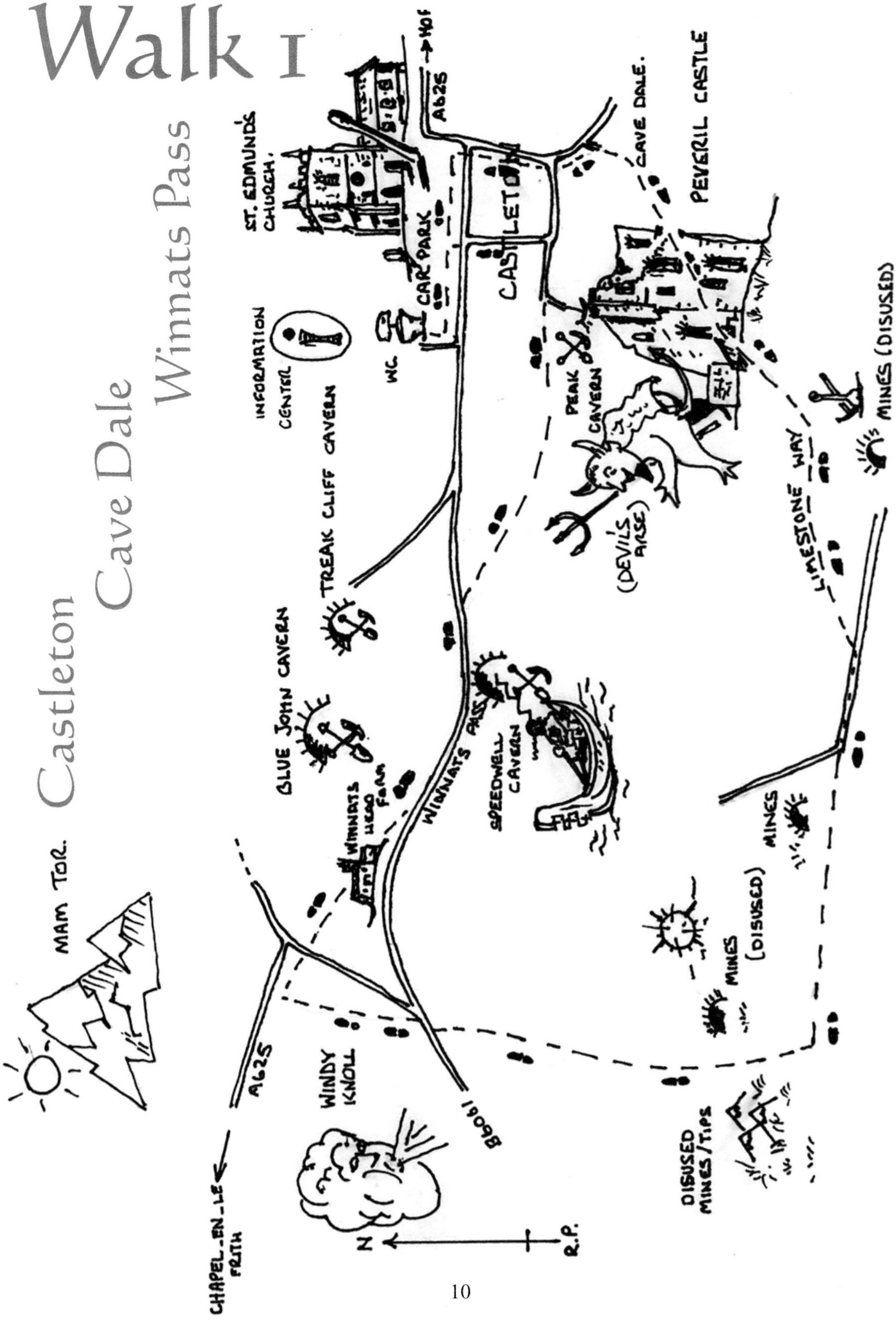

MAM TOR.
CHAPEL-EN-LE-FRITH
A625
BLUE JOHN CAVERN
TREAK CLIFF CAVERN
INFORMATION CENTER
ST. EDMUND'S CHURCH.
WINDY KNOLL
N
R.P.
WINNATS HEAD FARM
W.C.
CAR PARK
A625
→HOF
B6061
WINNATS PASS
SPEEDWELL CAVERN
CASTLETON
PEAK CAVERN
(DEVIL'S ARSE)
CAVE DALE.
PEVERIL CASTLE
DISUSED MINES/TIPS
MINES (DISUSED)
MINES
LIMESTONE WAY
MINES (DISUSED)

# Walk 1

## Castleton - Cave Dale - Winnats Pass

### About this walk

With stunning views, this rich and varied walk encompasses all that's best in the Peak District. Starting in the picturesque village of Castleton and passing close to Peveril Castle, the walk offers panoramic views over near and distant peaks, as well as the limestone gorges of Cave Dale and Winnats. You will pass close to three caverns, which could be visited in the course of the walk or after, if desired.

**Distance** 8.3km 5.2 miles

**Terrain** There is a steady ascent from Castleton through Cave Dale and part of this section is stony and uneven (the stunning views make the effort well worthwhile). After this stage, the way is generally either level or downhill. There is a long, steady descent through Winnats, on the return leg. Parts of the route can be wet and muddy. A varied terrain, including dales, fields, tracks, lanes, pavements and footpaths.

**Map** OS Outdoor Leisure 1 The Peak District, Dark Peak area. 1:25 000 scale.

**Starting Point** The large car park in Castleton (off A6187), next to National Park Information Centre (pay and display). Public toilets in car park.
Grid reference SK 149 829.

**Refreshments** Castleton offers a variety of pubs, cafés and shops.

1. From car park entrance, turn ***left*** into **Cross Street**

✓ **Castleton Centre (National Park information and visitor centre) is on your right**

2. Cross over road and shortly turn ***right*** into **Castle Street** (by **The Castle** inn)

✓ **Peveril Castle is named after William Peveril, believed to have been an illegitimate son of William the Conqueror. His castle played an important role in guarding the Forest Peak area, which was valuable for its lead, silver and hunting grounds. By the 17th century the castle had fallen into disrepair, only the keep was in use, as a courthouse. When this was abandoned, the castle deteriorated, until its remains were restored in the 19th century. The castle is now in the care of English Heritage.**

3. At top of **Castle Street**, turn ***left*** and continue up hill (past memorial cross and **Market Place**)
4. Shortly, as road bears left, turn ***right*** between cottages (where **Bargate** ends and **Pindale Road** begins)
5. Follow lane up into **Cave Dale**

✓ **Note the interesting information board in the entrance to Cave Dale.**

6. Go over stile by gate and follow path up dale for some distance

7. Near top of wide track, go through gate on right. Then head straight across and through gate in wall opposite

8. Very shortly, turn ***left*** and head diagonally up hill to top right-hand corner of field

9. Go through gap at side of gate and carry on (wall on both sides). Very shortly, go over stile by gate

10. Immediately, go over stile on right and follow lane (wall on both sides)

11. Shortly, as lane turns sharp right, go over stile by gate and carry straight on along track to opposite wall. Go through stile by gate and continue

12. After a short time, turn ***right*** over stile (look out for gate on left and gate in front of you) and then head up field (wall on left)

13. Shortly, go over further stile and continue (wall on left-hand side) to wall opposite

14. Go over stile near corner and carry on down (wall on left-hand side)

*Winnats Pass*

✓ **Mam Tor, ahead in the distance, is 517 m (1696 ft) high. Its name means 'Heights of the Mother'. It is also known as the Shivering Mountain because its lower shale layers are unstable and constantly crumbling. Encircling the summit was a late Bronze Age and early Iron Age hill fort. The earliest remaining features are two Bronze Age burial mounds, one just below the summit and the other on the summit itself.**

15. Near to farm, follow path as it bears diagonally right to right-hand corner of field
16. Go through gate, turn ***right*** and almost immediately cross road and go through small gate by large one
17. Carry straight on (wall on left). As wall ends, keep on towards wall opposite
18. Ignore first track on right (this leads to **Windy Knoll Cave**). Turn ***right*** just before wall and gate (almost heading back on yourself).
19. Follow path to wall opposite (**Winnats Head Farm** in distance ahead)
20. Go through gate, cross road and through gate opposite. Head straight across field to further gate opposite
21. Continue straight on (wall and farm on right)

✓ **On the left is Blue John Cavern, one of four show caves in Castleton. Blue John is a semi-precious mineral, claimed to be found only at Castleton. The mineral is found in veins in the limestone deep within the Blue John Cavern, where it has been mined for centuries. The Romans were the first to discover Blue John some 2,000 years ago. This cavern is open to the public.**

22. Carry on down past farm (road on right-hand side) and head down **Winnats Pass**

✓ **Hemmed in on both sides by limestone pinnacles, Winnats is thought to mean 'wind gates'. It formed a natural gateway to the fortified village of Castleton in medieval times. The pass is believed to have been the scene of the brutal murder of a young eloping couple in the late 18th century.**

23. Continue down for some time, passing through a couple of gates (keep road on right)
24. Towards bottom of **Winnats**, just past **Speedwell Cavern**, cross road and go through small gate by large one. Carry straight on (wall on left) to enter **Long Cliff**
25. Eventually, go over stile by gate and continue on
26. As path and wall go left downhill, ignore path going up towards **Pevril Castle**. At end of path, go through gate and continue down track, past houses
27. Carry on, as track becomes lane (**Goosehill**). Go over small bridge and turn ***left*** to walk alongside stream
28. Cross road to reach car park

# Walk 2

## Edale - Pennine Way
## Upper Booth - Barber Booth

## Walk 2

# Edale - Pennine Way - Upper Booth - Barber Booth

### About this walk

A walk of stunning beauty in the Dark Peak. This area is one of the most dramatic landscapes of the National Park and is steeped in its history. Although the route includes a short stretch of the Pennine Way, the walk is unchallenging and is an excellent introduction to this wonderful area.

| | |
|---|---|
| **Distance** | 6.3km 4 miles |
| **Terrain** | Not a demanding walk, with steady rises only. A mixture of lanes, footpaths, tracks and quiet roadway. Some parts of the Pennine Way are paved and the route is generally sound and fairly even underfoot. |
| **Map** | OS Outdoor Leisure 1 The Peak District, Dark Peak area. 1:25 000 scale. |
| **Starting Point** | The large Derbyshire Dales car park in Edale village, by the railway station (pay and display). Public toilets in car park.<br>Grid reference SK 124 853. |
| **Refreshments** | Edale offers a variety of pubs, cafés and a Post Office. |

1. Leave car park through side exit by toilets. Go down steps and turn ***right***
2. Walk up road, under railway bridge and continue along road for some time, past the **Moorland Centre**, **Edale Church** and into village

✓ **The Moorland Centre has a living roof of sedum turf, split by a waterfall flowing over glass panels into a pool at the entrance. The turf forms an eco-friendly insulator, and the building is fuelled by an energy-saving ground-source heat pump. Inside, interactive exhibitions show what the Moors for the Future Project is all about.**

3. Just past school and before **The Old Nags Head**, turn ***left*** (ignore footpath directly opposite school). Walk a short distance and go through gateway

✓ **On Good Friday 1954, the Peak District National Park Voluntary Warden Service (renamed the Ranger Service in 1974) was officially inaugurated outside the Nags Head Inn.**

4. Follow path up hill (small stream soon appears on right)
5. Near top of path, go through gate. Very shortly, turn ***left***, go through gate and follow paved path, slightly right, to opposite wall

✓ **This is the start of the Pennine Way, the first and longest footpath in England, opened in 1965.**

6. Pass through gated stile and continue on, passing through a further 5 stiles or gates (keep valley on left). Ignore paths off
7. Continue on and, as valley comes into view in distance ahead, follow path down (between 2 small hillocks)

8. Soon, cross over stile, turn ***left*** and continue down
9. Pass through small gate and bear slightly diagonally right
10. Go through gap by 2 old stone posts. With these stone posts to your back, bear left and continue down to bottom of field
11. Cross stile by large gate (ignore large gate on left). Walk down track towards **Upper Booth Farm**

✓ **In mediaeval times, there were herdsmen's shelters or 'booths'. These are now the hamlets of Upper Booth, Barber Booth, Ollerbrook Booth and Nether Booth. The central 'booth' was Grindsbrook Booth - now called Edale.**

12. Go through small gate by large one and turn ***left***. Almost immediately, turn ***left*** through small gate by large one with house opposite (do not go into farmyard)
13. Go straight across field, over small stream and through gate opposite
14. Walk slightly diagonally right to fence opposite. Go through gate (passing single stone post)
15. Continue on (fence/trees on right). Cross very small stone bridge (ignore gates on right) and carry on to right-hand corner of field
16. Cross small stream by little stone bridge, go through small gate and turn ***right***

*Visitor Centre, Edale*

17. Very shortly, go through small gate by large one and bear left to gate in middle of left-hand wall

18. Go through this gate and straight across field. As path becomes track, continue on (railway on right)

19. Soon, turn ***right*** and cross over railway-bridge. Follow track as it curves left, go through gate and on into farmyard

20. Walk to right-hand side of farm and follow lane straight on between houses (ignore lane to right)

21. Carry on past **Edale Methodist Chapel**. At T-junction, turn ***right*** and walk down lane to road

22. At road, turn ***right*** and cross bridge. Almost immediately, cross over road, turn ***left*** and cross stile by gate

23. Go straight up hill. On reaching top of slope, bear slightly right and continue to boundary of trees opposite

24. Go through trees and straight across field to tree boundary opposite

25. Cross stream and over stile. Bear slightly right and follow paved path to line of trees opposite (fence/hedge on right)

26. Go down steps into gully and cross stream. Go over stile, follow path to right and continue up

27. At top of far side of gully, bear slightly right and cross field (barn on right). Walk along right-hand side of wall

28. As line of trees bears off to left, carry straight on towards line of trees ahead

29. Go down steps, across stream and up steps to stile. Go over this stile (through line of trees)

30. Cross field towards another line of trees opposite (**Small Clough Farm** on left). Go through gateway

31. Cross field to opposite side, then cross stream and go over stile

32. Bear slightly right to gateway opposite. Head straight across field (**Hardenclough Farm** on left), over stile, down steps and turn ***left*** onto lane

33. Follow lane (river on right) past farm and eventually to road

34. On reaching road, turn ***right***, past houses and back to car park

# Walk 3

## Mam Tor
## Hollins Cross
## Edale

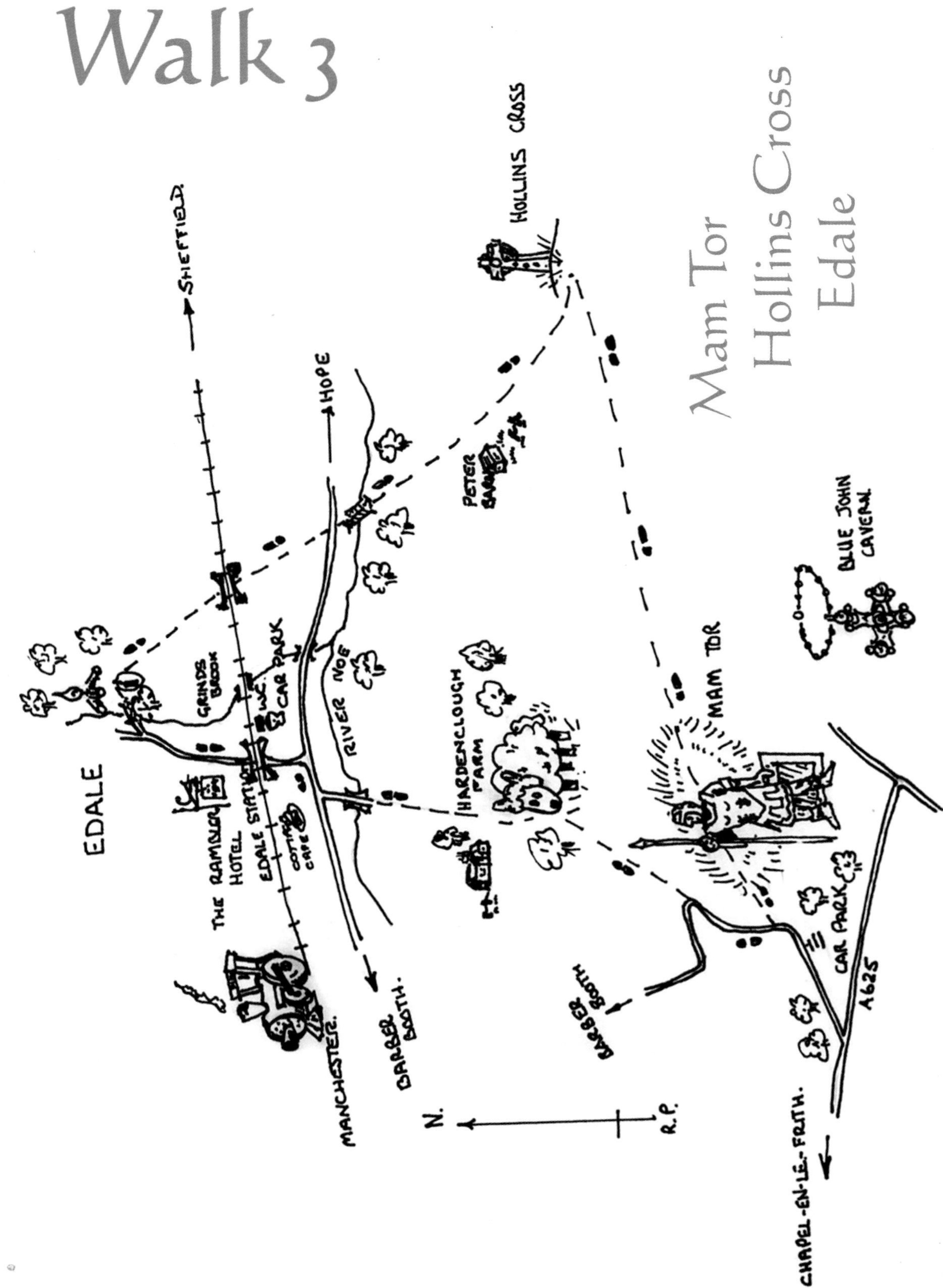

# Walk 3

# Mam Tor - Hollins Cross - Edale

## About this walk

This is a walk of spectacular and panoramic views, well worth the effort of the stepped climb to the summit of Mam Tor. Although relatively short, the route is one of great contrast, from the dramatic, rocky summit to the lush Vale of Edale. Best done on a clear day to appreciate the stunning and varied countryside all around.

**Distance** 6.3km 4 miles

**Terrain** A slightly demanding walk with 2 steep ascents, one to reach the summit of Mam Tor and the other to return to the car park. The descent from Hollins Cross into the valley is fairly rough and uneven underfoot. A mixture of footpaths, tracks, lanes and quiet roadway.

**Map** OS Outdoor Leisure 1 The Peak District, Dark Peak area. 1:25 000 scale.

**Starting Point** National Trust car park (pay and display). Drive through Castleton on A6187 (from direction of Hope). Just beyond Castleton village, turn left towards Speedwell Cavern. Follow road up through Winnats Pass. At T-junction turn right and then next left. Car park is appox. 500m on right.
Grid reference SK 123 832.

**Refreshments** Edale offers a variety of pubs, cafés and a Post Office.

1. Go up steps at top left-hand side of car park
2. From top of steps, follow path and go through gate on right, by road. Continue up further steps to summit of **Mam Tor**

✓ **Mam Tor is 517 m (1696 ft) high. Its name means 'Heights of the Mother'. It is also known as the Shivering Mountain because its lower shale layers are unstable and constantly crumbling.**
**Encircling the summit was a late Bronze Age and early Iron Age hill fort. The earliest remaining features are two Bronze Age burial mounds, one just below the summit and the other on the summit itself.**
**Wonderful views over the valleys of Hope and Edale.**

3. From summit, head down paved path and then along ridge, passing through a couple of gates
4. As path starts to rise (by memorial stone), turn sharp ***left*** (almost back on yourself) and head down wide path
5. Shortly, as path forks, take right-hand path down hill towards bottom of **Vale of Edale**
6. Continue down (path becomes less defined) towards wall at bottom (farm buildings over on right). Go through small gate down to farm track
7. Turn ***left*** along track, go past barn (**Peter Barn**), over stile by gateway and continue down

8. At end of track, cross stile by gate, go over small bridge (over **River Noe**) and, as track bends right towards house, take small path straight up to road

9. Go through gate, cross road and through gate opposite

10. Walk up side of field (wall on left). 2/3 of way up field, go through gate and stile on left and head diagonally right towards railway bridge

11. Go under bridge and straight on up. At corner of field, go through stile and diagonally right to right-hand side of barn

12. Go through stile and continue straight on (river over to left)

13. At stone bridge on left, go through stile by gate, cross bridge and follow path (by graves) up to road

❖ **If you wish to visit Edale village, turn right. Return to this point, continue on past Moorland Centre and carry on from instruction 15.**

14. Turn ***left*** along road

✓ **The Moorland Centre has a living roof of sedum turf, split by a waterfall flowing over glass panels into a pool at the entrance. The turf forms an eco-friendly insulator, and the building is fuelled by an energy-saving ground-source heat pump. Inside, interactive exhibitions show what the Moors for the Future Project is all about.**

15. Pass **Moorland Centre** on left, continue on past **The Rambler Hotel** on right and under railway bridge

✓ **Edale Cottage Café is along a lane to your right and on your left is a large car park with public toilets.**

16. Carry on along road and at T-junction turn ***right***

17. Shortly, turn ***left*** into lane (leading to **Hardenclough Farm**). Cross bridge and continue

18. Carry on past farm on right, through gate or over stile and continue up lane

19. Keep to lane as it meanders along for some distance

20. Near top of lane (just by house on right) go through gate on left and turn immediately ***right*** along path

21. Follow path up hill for some time, passing through 2 gates (at time of writing)

22. Finally, on reaching road, go through gate and turn ***left*** up road. As road bends to right (bottom of **Mam Tor**), cross over and turn ***right*** to go down steps to car park

# The Miller's Dale Walks

*River Wye, Miller's Dale*

*Old mill wheel*

*Anglers Rest*

*St. Anne's*

# The Lime Worker's Tale

My brother Ed's wife seems to be shelling them like peas. Six, to date, and they've only been wed as many years. All the shine's gone off her now, which is what you'd expect. I was telling him just the other day - supping a pint in the Anglers Rest, the pair of us, as we quite often do of an evening - that he needs to take things a bit easier there. That poky railway cottage of theirs can't hold many more.

It won't be me, getting landed with all of that. Turned twenty-five last month, still a single man and going to keep it that way for a few years longer, if possible. No girl's got under my skin yet, in any case, and no one's come crying to me that she thinks she's carrying, so we've got to be wed. Been lucky up to now, you could say.

At least Ed seems to be fond enough of what he's produced. Not like grandfather. I'd say for most of the time he hated the sight of the lot of us, and hadn't much time for Ma either, who was his only daughter. God only knows why she agreed to take him in. Perhaps she felt she hadn't any other choice. When grandmother died, Ma was the only one he still had, and of course he brought a few pennies along with him.

Mind you, for the man to have lived long enough to be a father was a miracle in itself, given what he'd been through. A good many of those he'd grown up with were dead and buried long before, so he must have been made of sterner stuff. A survivor the man was, no doubt at all of that, even if it had left him with a twisted back and a bent shoulder. He used to be in pain a lot of the time, especially by the end of a working day, but it wasn't just his body that had been wrecked, it was his mind, and more so. Couldn't get on with anybody, not for all the rest of his life, and he never trusted a soul. I know none of us ever chose to be in the same room as him, not if we could help it. One word out of place would get you a clout, and in any case, you always knew he didn't want you there. But with our own father dead, well - he was master of the house.

I hated the man, as a child, but in all honesty, if I look back, I can't condemn him. When he knew he was dying, he began to talk to me, just a bit. Not often, but more than he ever had in my seventeen years. And since then, I've spoken with a couple of others who managed to live through it. Their tale's the same as his. Just the same.

He reckoned he must have been about five, when he was dumped at a Poor House in London. That'd make it around 1798. Was born a bastard, most likely, with a mother who couldn't cope any longer, or perhaps she fancied her own chances a bit better without a child. He could barely remember that place, though what he did remember, very clearly, was being shoved, one freezing day, on to a wagon, along with a load of others. All of them huddling together as the thing lurched and rocked along. A few days later, they land up at Litton Mill, a couple of miles from here. Not that he'd have had a clue where he was back then. Place was owned by a bastard, in the way you'd damn well mean the word - Ellis Needham. That man's been dead for many years, but a lot of folk around here still spit on the ground at the mention of him.

Grandfather must have been seven when he started at that place. Him and all the others, none of them much older. Apprentices, they were called - what a nasty joke of a word. Kept like animals. Cramped, cold, half-starved. It's all been written about now - go and look it up for yourself, if you're not inclined to believe me. A lot of them died of infection and disease, hardly a surprise. Their sleeping place - it was named the Apprentice House - was filthy, a cramped rat heap of damp old blankets. And you don't have the strength to stay well, when you're living on watery porridge, or a bit of broth and the odd stale oatcake. But then, losing a good number of his apprentices was no problem for Ellis Needham. There were plenty more to be had, from the same place or from others. No end of boys - and girls, as well - to be had for free. City authorities were glad enough to be rid of them. Some of the luckier ones ended up at Cressbrook Mill and that's also quite close by. Far better treated there, than in that slave house of Ellis Needham.

Needham even buried the poor wretches in different graveyards, to avoid too much local talk. He only expected one thing from them, of course. Years of hard labour in his damn cotton mill. Fifteen hours a day and plenty of lashes if anyone loitered about or chatted or couldn't wait long enough to relieve themselves. Children had weights hung down their backs, to teach them a lesson or two. That's probably what did for Grandfather's back.

I'd have dearly loved to learn that Needham had been hung from a gibbet, and been well lashed before he got there. Didn't happen, of course - the bastard died in his own bed. But at least he'd managed to lose his fortune. Went bankrupt in the end and finished life as a pauper, so I heard. Wasn't a bad enough fate for him.

Anyway, that's a long time ago. Grandfather died about eight years back, and he'd lived to a very good age, despite everything - not far off eighty. He'd seen his wife off to a much earlier grave, and two of his children as well. There's still five of us grandchildren, but only me who ever gives the man a kindly thought.

He was set free at the age of twenty-one and found a bit of work around here, farm labouring. Got himself married within a couple of months. She was a young widow - only one child, and a cottage in Miller's Dale village. Tiny place, but decent. He caught her when she was still raw and grieving, no doubt fretting about how she was going to get by without a breadwinner. And he hadn't lived through fourteen years at Litton Mill without finding out how to look after himself. So he made sure he got her. She took him in, deformed or not. I'd wager she often rued the day.

He was a hard worker, you've got to give him that. Couldn't be anything else, laziness had been beaten out of him. And I'm not a bad labourer myself, either, as it happens. Used to do much the same as him, up to a couple of years ago - worked for farmers, any jobs they had going. Even built their kilns for them - a few farmers still had their own then, to make lime for the land and then sell a bit on. I kept the cursed things alight and raked lime out from all the nasty, spitting, scorching embers. No easy job, but I was good and quick with it, so it was a simple enough step to get better paid work at the big kilns when they opened up, just down the dale. Two years back, that was, in 1878. Built just above the railway line, right into the rock face. It's only the railway that means the things can be the size they are. Lime can be shovelled out of them by the ton-load, wheeled off in barrows and then tipped straight down into the wagons. Then away it goes, to be used in God knows how many industries. They can never get too much of the stuff.

Damn hard graft, that is, don't be fooled into thinking anything else. Mostly I'm a drawer - or piker, as it can be known - shovelling and raking burning hot lime and ash out from the bottom of the kiln. Out of the 'eyes', as we call them. It's back-breaking, the heat's overpowering and you can't stop - there's the burners, chucking coal and chunks of limestone into the top of the kiln all the time, and just me and a lad working at the bottom. Then there'll be a couple of pickers to the side of us, separating quicklime out from the hot ash, getting it ready for the wagons. We've all got ourselves burnt, from time to time, and this stuff's evil - much worse than any ordinary burn. You learn to take care, but every now and then there'll be a bad accident, even a death. Usually when someone's taken a few too many drinks. Not a wise thing at all, that.

Ed works for the railway - the Midland. Repairs tracks and does general maintenance. Looks like a steady job, and just as well with that family of his. Before the railway came through this dale, back in the sixties, Miller’s Dale village wasn't what you'd call a place at all. Handful of cottages, Anglers Rest, that was it. Nothing close by but a few more scattered cottages and run-down farms. It's not a lot bigger now, I'll grant you, but it's on the mainline to Manchester and - even more important - it's got its own line up to Buxton. And that means hordes of people - fairly well-to-do people in the main - have to change trains here, at Miller's Dale Station. Because Buxton's getting more and more to be the place to take a trip to, especially for people who want to spend their time and money sitting in warm spa water, and all such damn nonsense. So that town's growing all the time, new hotels and lodging houses opening up and the trains getting busier by the month. If there comes a day when I've had enough of lime kilns, I'll no doubt look for work with the Midland myself.

As it is, I can get myself over to Buxton easily enough, on the train. Better than walking two miles to Tideswell, and far more pretty girls around the town to have look at. It's rare that I let on to them where I live. Quite nice to climb into a carriage and head back down to Miller's Dale, at the end of a day. Or else get the first train in the morning, if the night's been a long one. The Midland railway station, in Buxton, is a very smart building indeed, not a bad place to hang around for a bit. It's right next door to another station that looks exactly the same, a mirror image. That one belongs to the London and North Western Railway - the two of them were in a race to get their lines to Buxton and as it turned out they opened up their stations on the same day, back in 1863. That just shows you how popular the town was getting to be. But only the Midland comes through Miller's Dale.

A sister of mine, Ellen, is in Buxton. Lives in, at one of the big hotels there - St. Anne's, on The Crescent. Maid of all work, from what I can gather, but she says she's getting trained to help in the Women's Bath, as a personal attendant. People pay a fortune to stay at that place and sit for an hour or two in the warm water, which Ellen tells me comes from a spring near the hotel. There's a good few of these springs, but it's thought they must all come from one place, very deep below the ground, because the water's always exactly the same temperature - never changes. I know well enough that what Ellen was really hoping for, when she managed to get a position there - about eighteen months back - was to meet a rich man. Or at the least a comfortably-off one. But the problem is, most men who stay at that place are already married, and quite old into the bargain. And out in the town or in the Pavilion Gardens, there's a fair bit of competition for any well-to-do single types. So she looks like ending up with one of the bath hands at a hotel close by, The Central. Not what she wanted of course, but she's not far off twenty-four now. When I saw her with him, just the once, the fact that it's not what she wanted was written all over her. That poor fellow's in for a wretched life, no matter that she's got a pretty face. Can't believe he doesn't see it, isn't looking beyond the nice skin and the firm breasts. That'll all be gone within three or four years, if Ed's lass is anything to go by.

If you're wandering around Miller's Dale village now, you certainly won't have got here aboard a train, although your car may well be parked at the old railway station. This place is almost unknown once again, now that the main line and its Buxton branch are barely even a memory. The railway viaduct serves as a path for walkers, or otherwise the enormous thing would have been ripped down by now. Our old Anglers Rest can still serve a pint, but the big lime kilns are abandoned, silent. They're only a short walk from the station, along the old track, if you'd care to take a look at them. There's even a bit of information there about how they used to be. Though it might well be hard, now, to imagine the acrid smell of burning lime and coal, the dense smoke, the heat, the showering sparks. Or to hear the ghost of men's shouts and curses, against the hissing of a steam engine on the track below.

No need to hang around there too long. The things are only empty shells. Amble on, along the overgrown Miller's Dale. I doubt very much that its quiet will be broken by the rattle of trains, ever again.

## Historical Note

Miller's Dale is now a delightful area of the Peak District, so it is perhaps hard to imagine that in the latter part of the 19th century it was a real hive of industrial activity.

The Midland Railway's main line came through this dale, from where a branch line went up to Buxton, a spa town of growing popularity. Miller's Dale Station itself, therefore, was a busy and important junction, especially in summer. At one time, it was unusual in having a post office on one of its platforms. The station closed in 1968, and its old ticket office is now used as a base for the Peak Park Ranger Service.

The coming of the trains in 1863 also encouraged other industries in Miller's Dale. Huge lime kilns were built close to the railway line, and limestone quarries in the immediate area were much expanded. The dale must have been full of noise, smoke, shouting and bustle - vastly different from the quiet and rather remote atmosphere it has today.

It is a fictional character who tells this tale, but the nature and details of his hard-working life are authentic, as is also his description of Litton Mill. That place was, at one time, notorious for appalling treatment of its young workers. This was gradually to come to public attention, and may even have inspired Dickens in writing 'Oliver Twist'.

# Walk 4

## Miller's Dale Station
## Limestone Way
## Wormhill

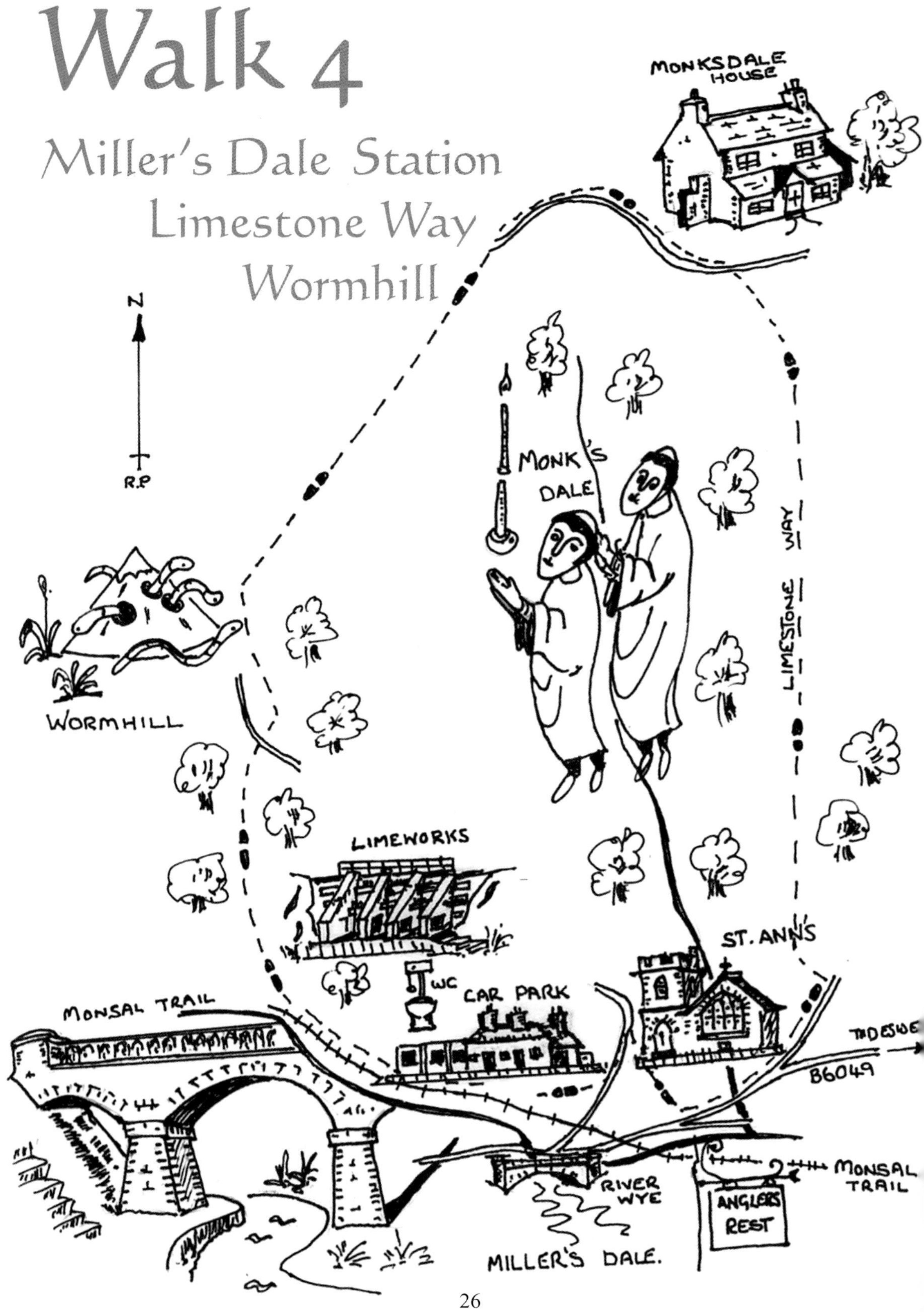

# Walk 4

# Miller's Dale Station - Limestone Way - Wormhill

## About this walk

This is an attractive and varied walk, with a mixture of wide, rolling views, dales, villages and riverside. To this can be added not only the interest of the old railway and lime kilns, but also the fascinating flora of Miller's Dale.

| | |
|---|---|
| **Distance** | 8km 5 miles |
| **Terrain** | Not an overly demanding walk, but a couple of longish pulls and one moderate descent. Just before reaching car park, at end of walk, there is a short but steep ascent up steps by old railway viaduct. |
| **Map** | OS Explorer OL24 The Peak District, White Peak area. 1:25 000 scale. |
| **Starting Point** | Peak District National Park car park. From A6(T) turn onto B6049 (signposted Blackwell) and follow into Miller's Dale. Take first left on entering village (signposted Wormhill), under two bridges and left again very shortly, into car park of old railway station (pay and display). Public toilets on platform. Grid reference SK 139 733. |
| **Refreshments** | Miller's Dale village has a pub, the Anglers Rest. In summer there is often a refreshment van in station car park. |

1. From old station car park, return through main entrance and turn ***left*** up road

✓ **The station at Miller's Dale was an important junction on the Midland Railway Line. The original station, with three platforms, opened in 1863 and served the main line for London and Manchester, with a branch line to Buxton. A further two platforms were added when the second viaduct was opened in 1905. Farmers from all over the Peak came to the station every morning to catch the 'Milk Train' which took their milk to bottling plants. Hundreds of day-trippers poured off the trains from the industrial areas during the summer months.**
**The railway closed in 1968, and remained unused for twelve years, before the Peak National Park acquired it.**

2. As road bends left, in front of **Glebe Farm**, turn ***right*** over stile in wall
3. Continue through gateway into **Monk's Dale** and carry on down
4. On meeting wall ahead, turn ***right*** through wooden gate, then down a few steps. Go by church and turn ***left*** up road

✓ **Just opposite St. Anne's Church, is a small road leading to the original wheel of an old meal mill, with information board. Just a little further on is the Anglers Rest Inn.**

❖ **If you wish to visit the above, cross over road in front of church. Afterwards, return to instruction 5.**

5. Very shortly, go over bridge and immediately bear left, past houses and up lane

*Lime kilns, Miller's Dale*

6. Shortly, turn ***left*** (almost turning back on yourself) along **Limestone Way**
7. Go through gate, continue into farmyard and turn ***left***, go through further gate on right-hand side of farmhouse
8. Continue further up this track for some distance as it twists and turns, passing through further gate(s). Continue as track bears sharp left, ignore track going straight ahead (ignore footpaths off)
9. Eventually, on meeting road, turn ***left*** and follow road down
10. Continue as road goes downhill and then bears left. At bottom of dip, ignore paths on left and right (to **Monk's Dale**)
11. As road begins to rise, go through small stile in wall on left
12. With your back to stile, head slightly diagonally right up field
13. At top corner of field, go through stile or gate and continue up (wall on both sides)

14. Eventually, at T-junction, turn ***right*** and head up track (wall on both sides). Keep to track, ignoring all paths off
15. Go through stile by gate and continue ahead (ignore stile in wall immediately on left)
16. Pass through further gate and continue along winding track
17. Just before houses, turn ***left*** over stile in wall (near gate) and cross to stile opposite
18. Go through this stile, continue straight on (wall on left, farm buildings on right) and go over stile in wall opposite

✓ **The Hamlet of Wormhill is just to your right.**

19. Carry straight on, passing through 3 more stiles and continue along track (ignore path off to left by 3rd stile)
20. At T-junction, turn ***left*** (walls on both sides)
21. Go through gate and head diagonally left across field (further up than stone building)
22. Cross stile in wall, to right of gateway. With your back to stile, head diagonally left across field to bottom left corner
23. Go through stile and turn ***right***. Go over stile by gate and straight on (wall on right)
24. As wall ends, carry straight on (wall now on both sides)
25. Go through small gate, down a few steps and straight on down track
26. Pass first building, go down right-hand side of second building and across garden to opposite wall and road
27. Go over stile, down steps and turn ***right*** up road
28. Just past first entrance on right, turn ***left*** and walk down track, past house
29. Go through gate (into nature reserve) and carry on down
30. Continue on, as path opens out and bears left. Follow path as it starts to drop down towards **River Wye**
31. At bottom of track, on meeting river, go through small gate, turn ***left*** (ignore bridge ahead) and continue along riverside
32. Eventually, on meeting high bridge ahead, turn ***left*** up steps

✓ **The viaduct ahead was built for the old Midland Railway. It is frequently used for abseiling.**

33. On meeting track (former railway line), turn ***left*** and go past lime kilns and quarry

✓ **During the 19th century there was a huge demand for quicklime for the chemical, steel and agricultural industries. To meet this demand, many limestone quarries and kilns were opened by railway lines. Coal could be easily brought in and the processed quicklime taken away.**

34. Continue along track to reach car park

# Walk 5

Litton
Cressbrook Dale
Tansley Dale
Litton Edge

# Walk 5
# Litton - Cressbrook Dale - Tansley Dale - Litton Edge

## About this walk

This is a walk of two distinct parts, based around the attractive village of Litton. The first part leads you through farmland and meadows to the dramatic Cressbrook and Tansley Dales. The second part takes you above the village to Litton Edge, with wonderful views and rolling countryside.

| | |
|---|---|
| **Distance** | 7.2km 4.5 miles |
| **Terrain** | The route involves a couple of steepish but steady ascents out of the dales. For a short stretch, just before the descent into Cressbrook Dale, the path is narrow and a little tricky underfoot. Otherwise, the mixture of footpaths, tracks, lanes and quiet roads is reasonably sound underfoot. |
| **Map** | OS Explorer OL24 The Peak District, White Peak area. 1:25 000 scale. |
| **Starting Point** | The village school in Litton. Car parking on road or, if available, in front of school.<br>Grid reference SK 164 751. |
| **Refreshments** | Red Lion Inn and Litton Village Shop and Post Office. The shop serves hot drinks, homemade cake and snacks. Open seven days a week 8.30am-11.30am and 2pm-6pm Monday to Friday. Weekends 10am-4pm. |

1. With your back to village school, cross road, turn ***left*** and walk alongside road

✓ **When Litton's only shop was closed, the Post Office was rehoused in the Village Hall, but the villagers were not happy with this arrangement. They formed a friendly society and each villager bought a ten-pound share. What had once been the village smithy was converted into a shop, Post Office and meeting place for the community.**

2. Shortly, turn ***right*** along road, towards **Cressbrook** and **Monsal Dale** (if you pass Methodist Church, you've gone too far)
3. As lane bears right, turn ***left*** along wide track. Almost immediately, go over stile in wall on right
4. Head straight down field to stile in opposite wall. Cross this stile and head diagonally left to go over stile in left-hand wall (approx. 1/3 of way along wall)
5. With your back to stile, bear diagonally right, up to far right-hand corner of field
6. Go through stile near corner, cross wide track and over stile opposite
7. With your back to stile, head diagonally left to stile in middle of left-hand wall. Cross this stile and head diagonally right to gap in wall at top corner of field
8. From gap, head diagonally left, up to stile in top left corner. Go through stile and again head diagonally left to small gate near trees
9. Go through gate, turn ***right*** and take path along hillside (wall on right)

*Litton Village*

10. Continue along path as it eventually goes down steps. As path curves right, continue down to meet wide track
11. Turn ***left*** along this track (after a while it becomes a narrower path). Continue along path, passing through ruined wall, and carry on down into **Cressbrook Dale**
12. At bottom of dale, as path meets another, turn ***left*** along this path. Almost immediately, cross small bridge on right. Go along path and continue as path heads up (ignore path to left, running alongside river)
13. Eventually, at top of hill, take path bearing left back down to **Cressbrook Dale**
14. At bottom of dale, continue along (wall on left). On reaching large 'stepping stones' on left, cross over and go through small gate in wall ahead
15. From gate, continue up path. Keep to main path, (which leads out of **Cressbrook Dale** into **Tansley Dale**)

✓ **Many of the lumps and bumps in the ground are the remains of lead mining activities. These are visible around many villages of the Peak, where workings dramatically changed the landscape. Many old miners' paths are now public footpaths. Disused shafts were largely uncapped until fairly recently. Over the centuries, many lives were lost in these death traps.**

16. Continue as path eventually bears right and steeply up. Cross stile in corner (by gateway) and continue up path as it heads diagonally right
17. Carry on past corner of wall, then head for stile in far left-hand corner

18. Go over this stile and turn ***left*** along track. Very shortly, go over step stile in right-hand wall

19. Bear diagonally left to far left-hand corner of field. Cross stile (by house), turn ***right*** and walk to road

❖ **If you wish to finish the walk early, then turn left here into village. To break your journey with a stop for refreshments, do as above, then return here and continue the walk from point 20.**

20. Cross road and turn ***right*** (away from village). Just before road bears left, turn ***left*** up track (heading back on yourself)

21. Go over stile by gateway and carry on up field. Head through gap in wall at top right-hand side of field and continue up (keep near left-hand wall)

22. Go over stile in top left-hand corner of field, then straight on to bottom of field (wall on left)

23. Go over stile in wall and then across to stile in wall opposite

24. Cross a further 3 fields and stiles, then continue on (wall on left)

25. As path starts to descend, head diagonally right to bottom right-hand corner of field (by detached house)

26. Go over stile on left, near corner, then turn ***left*** and walk up lane

27. As lane meets road, at T-junction:

❖ **If you wish to return directly to the village, turn left along road to start of walk at village school. Otherwise, continue with walk from instruction 28.**

28. Cross road and head along grassy path opposite (wall on both sides)

29. On meeting road, turn ***left*** and walk back to village centre, past **Red Lion Inn** to start of walk

✓ **The Red Lion Inn first opened as a public house in 1787. Before this, the building had been part of a farm.**

*Litton Village Shop and Post Office*

# Walk 6

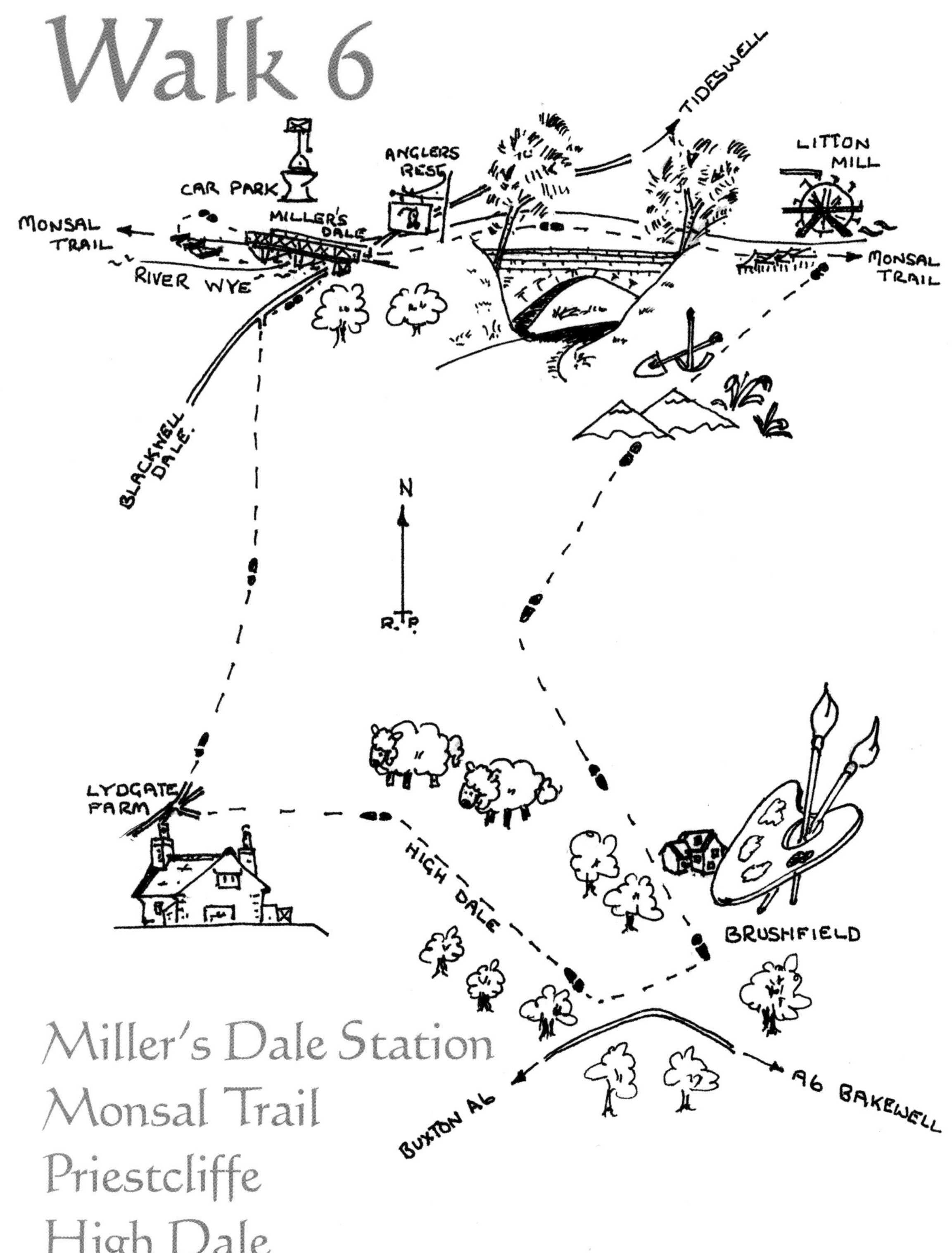


## Miller's Dale Station
## Monsal Trail
## Priestcliffe
## High Dale

# Walk 6

# Miller's Dale Station - Monsal Trail - Priestcliffe - High Dale

## About this walk

This is a beautiful walk, starting along the easy Monsal Trail and involving only one steep ascent. The rewards of this, however, in terms of wonderful views, make it well worth the effort. The walk offers a wide variety of scenery as well as some fascinating history and geology.

**Distance** 8.6km 5.3 miles

**Terrain** One long, steep, but manageable hill towards start of walk. After this the walk is mainly level or downhill, with only a few slight rises. Mainly good underfoot with a mixture of trail, footpaths, tracks, lanes and short stretch of roadside. Steps at end of walk to reach car park.

**Map** OS Outdoor The Peak District, White Peak area. 1:25 000 scale.

**Starting Point** Peak District National Park car park. From A6(T) turn onto B6049 (signposted Blackwell) and follow into Miller's Dale. Take first left on entering village (signposted Wormhill), under two bridges and left again very shortly, into car park of old railway station (pay and display). Public toilets on platform. Grid reference SK 139 733.

**Refreshments** Miller's Dale village has a pub, the Anglers Rest. In summer there is often a refreshment van in station car park.

1. From car park, go through gates into old station area (station and platform on right)

✓ **The station at Miller's Dale was an important junction on the Midland Railway Line. The original station, with three platforms, opened in 1863 and served the main line for London and Manchester, with a branch line to Buxton. A further two platforms were added when the second viaduct was opened in 1905. Farmers from all over the Peak came to the station every morning to catch the 'Milk Train' which took their milk to bottling plants. Hundreds of day-trippers poured off the trains from the industrial areas during the summer months. The railway closed in 1968.**

2. Walk forward a few paces, turn ***left*** and follow wide track (**Monsal Trail**) over railway bridge (look down on right for good view of **River Wye**). Continue past old lime kilns, shortly on right

❖ **If you wish to visit the lime kilns and read the information board, go up the steps (just beyond railway bridge).**

✓ **The lime works opened in 1878 and lime was transported by the Midland Railway. The lime produced was used in the chemical, steel and agricultural industries. Production here ended in 1930, when the quarry above became unstable and the rock face started to slip.**

3. Follow **Monsal Trail** for some distance (ignore paths off)

✓ **The Monsal Trail is the old Midland Railway track, now a walking route. It stretches from Wye Dale, near Buxton, to Bakewell. Most of the tunnels have been closed, but alternative routes have been provided. The trail and surrounding area has abundant wildlife, flora and fauna.**

4. Eventually, pass under footbridge, turn ***right*** immediately and go up stone steps
5. At top of steps, turn ***left***, go over stile and follow path up hill
6. Continue up hill as path bears diagonally right

✓ **Do glance occasionally at the view behind you. This hill is nature's way of making sure you look back to enjoy her work! From here Litton Mill can be seen, a small hamlet around a former cotton mill on the River Wye. The mill dates from the late 18th century and was notorious for the harsh treatment of its apprentices, many of whom were orphans from as far away as London. It may have inspired Dickens in writing Oliver Twist.**

7. Just over brow of hill, go over stile by large gate and continue up (wall/fence on right)
8. Near top of hill, turn ***right*** (ignore path to left) and go over stile. Turn ***left*** immediately and carry on up hill (wall on left)
9. Follow path as it turns right and walk beside left-hand wall. Carry on to bottom of field (ignore stile in left-hand wall halfway along)

✓ **Many of the lumps and bumps in the ground are the remains of lead mining activities. These are visible around many villages of the Peak, where workings dramatically changed the landscape. Many old miners' paths are now public footpaths. Disused shafts were largely uncapped until fairly recently. Over the centuries, many lives were lost in these death traps.**

10. On meeting wall, go through stile by gate and turn ***left*** immediately. Follow wide track for some time, passing through a couple of large gateways
11. Continue on down, past farm buildings on right, and through large gateway
12. Pass through another large gateway and follow lane as it winds down (houses on left)
13. Eventually (near bottom of hill), as road turns sharp left (back on itself), go straight on through small gate on left side of large gate
14. Follow path through **High Dale** for some time (wall on right, ignore paths or tracks off)
15. Eventually, just after dale curves left, go through stile and gate
16. With back to stile, walk a few paces slightly diagonally right, to corner of left-hand wall
17. Continue around side of hill (moving slightly away from wall). Follow path as it bears left to meet left-hand wall again
18. Just before end of field, go through small gate in left-hand wall. With back to gate, bear diagonally right and round corner of right-hand wall
19. Pass through derelict wall and through small gated stile in wall opposite

20. Cross 3 fields, passing through 2 gated stiles and over 1 other stile. With back to this last stile, bear slightly diagonally left and head across field to left-hand corner

21. Go over stile, turn ***left*** and through stile in wall opposite. From stile, turn ***right***, head up hill for a few paces, go over further stile in wall opposite

22. Turn ***left*** and follow wide track down. Very soon, just before track turns left, turn ***right***, go a short way and then over stile

23. Head up track (derelict walls both sides) past houses and over stile. Continue up, as footpath joins lane coming up from right

24. At buildings (**Lydgate Farm**), turn ***right*** and follow lane (buildings now on left)

25. Continue along lane for some time (ignore paths off to right). Eventually, as lane turns sharp right, go over stile ahead

26. Carry straight on (wall on left) and down hill

✓ **On a clear day, Tunstead Limestone works are visible in the distance ahead. The old Miller's Dale quarry and limekilns can be seen on the right.**

27. At bottom of field, go over stile, turn ***left*** and continue down lane. Soon, on meeting another lane (at T-junction), turn ***right*** and continue as lane winds down hill

28. On meeting road, cross over and turn ***right***. Follow road to **Miller's Dale**

29. On entering **Miller's Dale**, cross bridge and turn ***left*** (towards **Wormhill**)

30. Shortly, as road turns right, turn ***left*** (by large gate) and up stone steps. Car park is on right at top of steps

*Miller's Dale Viaduct from below*

# The Reservoir Walks

Ladybower Reservoir

Ladybower Inn

Tip's Memorial

Visitor Centre, Fairholmes

# The Vicar's Tale

Well - that's over and done with then. Thought a wave of emotion was going to get the better of me, about halfway through the thing, but thank God it didn't. Not quite. Wouldn't have looked too dignified for an old church minister to be seen in tears, to have need of a comforting arm around his stooped shoulders. And when all's said and done, it's not as if anybody has died. There's been many a funeral taken place in this building, but there wasn't one today. Not for a person, anyway.

Far from it, in fact, if you could go along with the words of His Grace, the Bishop of Derby, and he gave a good address, no doubt about it. You can see why some men end up in high office, while others remain vicars of small congregations throughout their lives. The Bishop wanted this final Evensong to be a celebration of all the years of worship in this lovely church - a church which, he now states, we have a duty to sacrifice. And never, in my forty-seven years here, have I seen the place so packed. Pushed together in every last bit of space they were, and spilling out of the door. People of this village and of several others, even a big group of hikers, out all the way from Sheffield. Plus, of course, a cartload of officials from the Water Board. What, one wonders, was going on in their minds? 'A sad event, but needs must' - I dare say that was the general sentiment. It's unlikely that any of them have lost sleep over it.

For the people who live here, of course, it's a very different story. This is a place few have ever moved from in their lives, not until now. People expected to be christened here, married here, and to bury their parents or grandparents in the churchyard. Not that this particular church goes back that far - it was built in 1867, to replace what was, so I gather, a cramped and very ugly chapel. But the history of worship in the valley goes back hundreds of years, and so does our village. What's left of it. This was the heart of what must surely be the most desolate and rugged parish in Derbyshire - Derwent and Hope Woodlands.

I feel truly sick at heart for this place. Far lower in spirits than the Bishop probably imagined, when we cheerily agreed that my task now - very late in life - is to support the people of Derwent, or at least those who remain. As large a number has already moved on to the new housing built for them down at Yorkshire Bridge, a few miles away. Good enough houses, bigger than some are used to, but all in neat rows, not in the least like a real village. Can't see myself getting over there too often. And in any case, I'm retired now, supposedly. Not too much to ask, is it, a few months before my eightieth? But the Bishop knows, as well as I do, that I can't spend the length of every day reading and listening to the wireless, or watering a few flowers. I need to be out and about, as I've always been. There's not a house or farm around here where I'm not welcomed in for a cup of tea. And I've always known which days the different women are to be found baking, so it makes good sense to pay them a visit when there's a chance of a nice bit of warm bread or a fresh oatcake!

As it happens, of course, there's a lot more than the death of this village, or the destruction of a few farms, to worry about at present, as you'll be only too aware. There's no shortage of real deaths, and all the fears and grief that wartime brings, even to the most picturesque of places. No escaping the horrors. And in fact there's a real worry here that the dams could make this whole valley very vulnerable to attack - a well justified fear, in my view, when you think of the damage that such an attack would inflict. Common sense says they've got to be a likely target. Supposedly this whole area is being looked after by the Sherwood Foresters, but I'm not at all sure that the couple of air-raid shelters they've ordered to be thrown up are protection enough. Not even with that smokescreen, which we're told will be triggered in case of alert. It's already been triggered once - a false alarm, thank God. The whole valley was smothered in thick smoke, you could barely see a foot in front of you and the stuff didn't clear for hours. I suppose that was reassuring in a way, but it certainly makes you realise we don't live in any safe, remote haven out here. Not any more.

The smokescreen set-up is controlled by a group of conscientious objectors, so I believe. Much safer job than fighting, it hardly needs to be said. And of course we've got Home Guard chaps, constantly patrolling over the moors, much of the day and all night long. Just how much good they can do is another thing. You have to admire them, though, because it's been freezing cold at night for months now - I've never known a winter any harder. Driving winds, full of hail and sleet, almost all the time. And they go straight off to their jobs with the Water Board the next day, there's no allowance given at all for catching up on a few hours sleep. Not enough workers on site any more for that, which is all very different from back in 1935, when this latest one was started. There was certainly no shortage of men ready to be employed on the new dam back then. I thought they might well be forced to put the whole thing on hold for the length of the war - however long that turns out to be - but they've been determined to push on with it. In fact, a good few German prisoners have been put on to work, though I heard there's been a couple who've tried to make their escape. Didn't get very far! I can't for the life of me understand why they'd want to attempt it. Working on the Ladybower isn't a bad way of getting yourself through the war.

There's a lot of people round here - and I'm one of them - who feel that this valley has already sacrificed more than enough. Howden and Derwent dams are just up to the north, and their reservoirs have drowned God knows how many acres of fine land and destroyed a good few farms. Those two were started just after the turn of the century, and built by a huge army of navvies. I should remember! I was chaplain to the navvy village of Birchinlee they built up there for them - right through till 1916, when the job was finished and the place was pulled down. Just as well I was a much younger man then, because that lot took a lot of energy, rather more than I was prepared to give, at the time. A pretty rough crowd, you'd have to say, though good-hearted enough if you took the trouble to get to know them, which I rarely did, in all honesty. But at least I christened them, married them and buried them, and as often as not took criticism or a lot of loud mouthing in return. The wives were even tougher than the men, it always seemed to me. If they didn't see eye-to-eye with you, they'd tell you so straight and clear, no niceties bothered with. I'm well used to the native women of the valley, and they can be direct enough, Heaven knows, but nothing like that tribe. No doubt a hard life, forever on the move, makes for a certain sort of woman, but it was all a bit too much for me at the time. Fortunately for them, they had an excellent missioner living there - George Sutton. He really was the life and soul of the place. I've got to admit, looking back, that he gave far more care to those navvies and their families than I ever managed, and for a lot less money. A very good man - he should have been made a proper minister of the Church. He never pretended to like me particularly, but he was always very respectful. I dare say he believed I got rather more in financial reward than I gave in service to that village. Perhaps it was the case. I've never claimed to be a saint, though there were times, with those people, when I felt I'd earned everything that came my way! At the end of the job, when the whole place was pulled down and they all dispersed - well - I'd say it was a relief in one way, though my income took a significant dip. But it had certainly been a real eye-opener to me. No doubt I'd led far too sheltered a life.

At all events, it now seems yet another reservoir is needed, thirty years or so after tearing up the valley to create those other two. The cities obviously have an unquenchable thirst. But this time, the damage to our lives has been even greater - unlike before, there are not only farms, but two villages, lying in what will soon be a huge bowl of chill, dark water. Derwent and Ashopton - both ancient, of picture-postcard charm, both of them the English country villages of everyone's imagination. Ashopton is already not much more than a heap of black mud and rubble, and a huge viaduct, intended to carry a main road across the water, looms over it. That little place will soon be lying even deeper than Derwent.

I intend to spend some time in the church later this evening - on my own. I'll wait till the crowd - still milling round what remains of the village - has wandered away. I've always thought of it as my church, though the Water Board has owned it for about six years now, since 1937. Once the decision was made to flood this part of the Derwent Valley, they had to start making moves. The Board paid just over eighteen thousand for the lot - church, churchyard and vicarage. It's been rented back from them since then, at a hundred and twenty pounds a year, and I've been told I'll be allowed carry on living in the vicarage for twenty pounds a year. Only for the time being, you'd suspect. Perhaps it will see me through whatever time I've got left, but if I'm still breathing in a year or two, then I shall probably have to move out. The house is a little distance away from the church, but barely beyond what will soon be the water line, and I doubt they'll want to leave it standing there for long. As for the churchyard, it's now rough and very over-grown, a real eyesore. There's been no reason whatever to tend it since the bodies were moved out.

Very unpleasant, that operation was. Not far off three hundred corpses to be unearthed, around three years ago. A fair number of them were members of those navvy families from Birchinlee, the rest were people of the parish. The whole thing was done behind big screens, though it still aroused a great deal of morbid curiosity, as you'd expect, and a lot of distress as well. When people lay a loved one to rest, they expect those remains to be left in peace.

The Board's plan was to make a new graveyard down at Yorkshire Bridge, which would have been appropriate as that's where a lot of village people are going to be living. It didn't prove to be possible, though, as some local resident decided he was having none of it and, as it turned out, the law stood in his favour. So the Water Board felt obliged to cough up for a big extension to the graveyard at Bamford Church, and most of the remains have been reburied there. But the whole operation was very disturbing. Not just a matter of raising coffins and transporting them, though that would have been unpleasant enough. Every single one had to be opened and its contents checked. I got involved as little as I could - the whole thing was overseen by the County Medical Officer of Health, a Mr Heath. He had to make a full written report on each one, and I imagine he was thoroughly relieved when the job was complete. It would have been even worse, of course, had this church been older. Before it was built, burials had always taken place at Hathersage. The interesting thing though, is that what Mr Heath saw inscribed on a gravestone did not always tally with what was actually found inside the grave. Rather unsettling, that was.

It may well be only a matter of days now before this church is reduced to rubble. Better that way, perhaps, because it's doomed, and to be inside it now is a great sadness, no longer a comfort. There's talk of leaving the tower standing, and letting the waters gradually reach towards it and surround it. An abandoned spire, out there like the mast of a stricken ship, destined gradually to rot away.

That other wonderful building - Derwent Hall - is already in ruins. The Water Board got its hands on that back in 1927, and you could say we've all been living on borrowed time ever since. Now Henry Boot and Sons are doing a very thorough demolition job. It seems a long time since all those girls, from Notre Dame, used it as a boarding school during the first couple of years of the war. Even with the dams so close, it must have seemed a lot safer than Sheffield, with its heavy industry and armament factories. And the girls certainly brought a bit of life to the valley. People got used to seeing them out for long walks, in their school uniform dresses, and calling in at the village post office - all blazers and panama hats and rather well-bred accents. A very different influx of people from that navvy lot at Birchinlee! But eventually, the staff found the isolated old building - cold and ill-lit - a bit too grim, and it was decided to risk the city once again. Since those nice young ladies and their rather poker-faced teachers have gone, the Hall has been used as accommodation for a few of the men working on the new site, but I'd hesitate to describe these as navvies. Times have moved on, nowadays people want to be more settled. There's a few huts down near the site and a handful of workers have taken lodgings in the village, but many seem to come in everyday. Those who haven't gone off to fight in the war, of course. But this project is seen as essential work, and it's not the type of thing that women can easily step into.

Our village school, of course, will soon be below the water. The day that closed, it ended any sense of real life in this place. There can't be many schools around where children are allowed to play out in the village at lunchtime! They were always quite safe and they knew to get back to the classroom on time, otherwise there'd be sharp words, or even a cane at the ready. Old Miss Bingham's been a teacher there nearly fifty years - even longer than I've been around here - she knows every single family, through several generations. And on Saturdays she'd always give her brother, George, a hand in his post office shop. He was never the brightest of sparks - couldn't cope if the place got busy.

I suppose I should be thankful that I still have some sort of task to do in my old age - encouraging people to get on with their lives, away from the growing pile of rubble that was once a village. But it's not an uplifting thing. I often wish I could get out on the moors, as I used to, and do a bit of rabbit shooting. Never needed to buy any shot, always plenty of farmers happy enough to supply me! But it's a long time since I've had the energy to be striding out up there, so there's no getting away from this depressing scene.

And of course I no longer have my wife to share things with, either. Lucy died just over four years ago, buried in Bamford on the seventh of January, 1939. Thank God that was after they'd stopped burials taking place here - I'd have found it appalling to have her dug up. As it happens, I was older than my wife by about eighteen years - never expected to be the one left on my own. It's a hard thing to come to terms with, though the one, small compensation is that I can now please myself what I do and when I do it. There's a good number of widows around here, who'll tell you that's compensation enough! But for men it's often a lot tougher, in my experience.

Well, the evening's drawing on. Almost the end of the seventeenth of March, year of Our Lord nineteen forty-three. This is a date I shan't easily forget. I'll go and say my own farewell now to the lovely Church of St. John and St. James and perhaps even shed, in private, the tears I managed to hold back before. A few valuable pieces will be sent away to other places of worship and our beautiful east window is to be given a home in Hathersage Church. The endowment itself is to be transferred to Frecheville, near Sheffield. That will pay for the building of a new church there, once the war's over. So perhaps the spirit of this place won't entirely be lost. I'll cross Millbrook, on my way back to the vicarage, for the last time, because I shall not return to the church tomorrow.

Before too long, the valves of the new Ladybower dam will be closed. From that moment, our valley will start to fill. It will fill slowly - perhaps almost imperceptibly at first - but surely, inexorably. I cannot imagine what this place will look like in years to come. Still beautiful, perhaps, in some very different way. But never more so than now, as the colours of the evening sky light up the spire of its church, and soften the edges of its broken buildings.

*By kind permission of Prof. Brian Robinson*

# Historical Note

Ladybower was the last of three great reservoirs to be created in the Upper Derwent Valley, and it is now a dramatic feature of the area's stunning scenery. Sadly, however, it was to drown two lovely peakland villages, Derwent and Ashopton, whose inhabitants were provided with new housing in the hamlet of Yorkshire Bridge. For the people of those villages, the loss of their homes and close community must have been particularly hard to bear, given that it took place during the turmoil of the Second World War.

This tale is told by Walter Rouse, who was vicar of Derwent and the scattered parish of Hope Woodlands for most of his working life. He retired, aged 79, after the last service to be held in Derwent Church, in March 1943. Reverend Rouse had served the area throughout the construction of Howden, Derwent and Ladybower dams, acting as chaplain to the navvy families of Birchinlee (known as 'Tin Town'), during the early years of the century.

*The viaduct rises above Ashopton*

*By kind permission of Prof. Brian Robinson*

# Walk 7

## Bridge End (car park)
## Lockerbrook Farm
## Derwent Reservoir

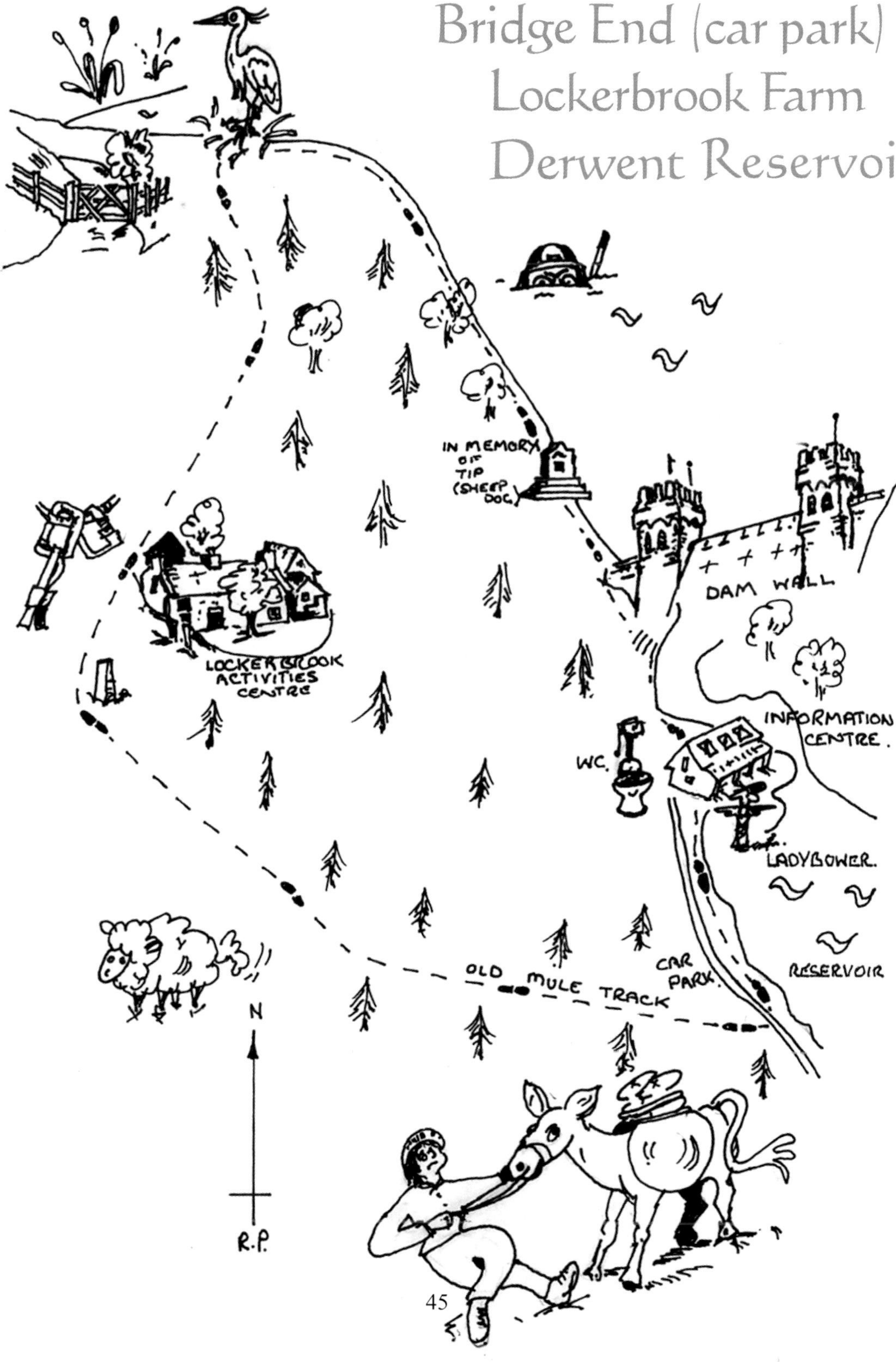

# Walk 7

## Bridge End (car park) - Lockerbrook Farm - Derwent Reservoir

### About this walk

A lovely walk in woodlands and across moorlands, with beautiful views over Derwent and Howden reservoirs to one side and the dramatic High Peak to the other. Not a particularly demanding walk, with a nice variety of terrain. Walk back along the reservoir and have a cup of tea at the attractive Fairholmes visitor centre!

| | |
|---|---|
| **Distance** | 7.6km 4.7 miles |
| **Terrain** | At start of walk, a longish, steady pull up a stony track. From this point, the way is fairly level or downhill. There is a mixture of woodland, footpaths, tracks and quiet lanes. Generally good underfoot. |
| **Map** | OS Outdoor Leisure 1 The Peak District, Dark Peak area. 1:25 000 scale. |
| **Starting Point** | Free parking in Bridge End car park. Travelling from the Bamford direction on A6013, cross the Ladybower Reservoir and turn left at the traffic lights onto A57. Cross the Ladybower Reservoir again and take the next right turn. After 1.5 miles the car park is on the left. Public toilets in National Park visitor centre near end of walk.<br>Grid reference SK 180 885. |
| **Refreshments** | Fairholmes National Park visitor centre and shop. Refreshments available, times vary according to season. |

1. From car park entrance, turn ***right*** and follow road. Very shortly, turn right through large gate
2. Follow wide track up hill (worth taking a breather, by looking at view behind you now and again). Eventually, at top of track, go through gate or over stile on right (ignore gate and stile to left) **(Phew! Don't worry, that's it for hills now)**
3. Carry straight on (trees to right). Eventually, near end of wood, go over stile

✓ **On your left, in the distance, are visible the summits of Lose Hill, Hollins Cross and Mam Tor. A 7th century battle is said to be commemorated in the names of Lose Hill and neighbouring Win Hill.**

4. Carry on, and very shortly turn ***right***. Continue on (woods on right)
5. Continue up (stone post on right). As path meets wide track, follow this track and eventually go past **Lockerbrook Outdoor Activity Centre**

✓ **The activity centre was once Lockerbrook Farm, built in 1756.**

6. Just beyond the activity centre, go through small gate by large one and continue up track (ignore steps to left)
7. As stone wall ends on right, ignore gateway on right (leading to **Fairholmes visitor centre**) and continue to follow track

8. Carry on as track starts to go down hill (ignore gate on right, again leading to **Fairholmes visitor centre**)

9. Follow wide track down for some distance, until track meets road. Go through large gate, cross road and turn ***right***

10. Walk along verge by road (reservoir on left). Continue past wall of dam

✓ **Howden and Derwent dams were constructed between 1901 and 1916 by a large army of navvy workers. Many of these lived in the specially constructed village of Birchinlee (known as 'Tin Town') on the edge of the Derwent reservoir. A claim to fame for Derwent reservoir is the link with the 'Dambuster' squadron of the RAF, which used it to practise for the famous 'bouncing bomb' raid on the Ruhr dams. It is worth a look at the information board by the dam.**

11. Very shortly, turn ***left*** down steps and follow path towards National Park visitor centre (as path splits, ignore left hand path down steps). On meeting road, turn ***left*** and very shortly turn ***right*** to the centre

❖ **If you do not wish to go to the visitor centre, then do not turn left down steps, but continue along roadside back to car park.**

✓ **This attractive visitor centre offers car parking, refreshments and toilets, with a National Park shop and information point.**

12. On leaving visitor centre, head up to main road, turn ***left*** and follow road back to **Bridge End** car park on right

❖ **Shortly, on left, is a footpath (at end of small off road parking area), which also leads to Bridge End car park. This is a pleasant route away from the road, which can be walked as an alternative.**

*Looking across Ladybower from car park*

# Walk 8

## Cutthroat Bridge - Grindle Barns
## Ladybower - Ashopton

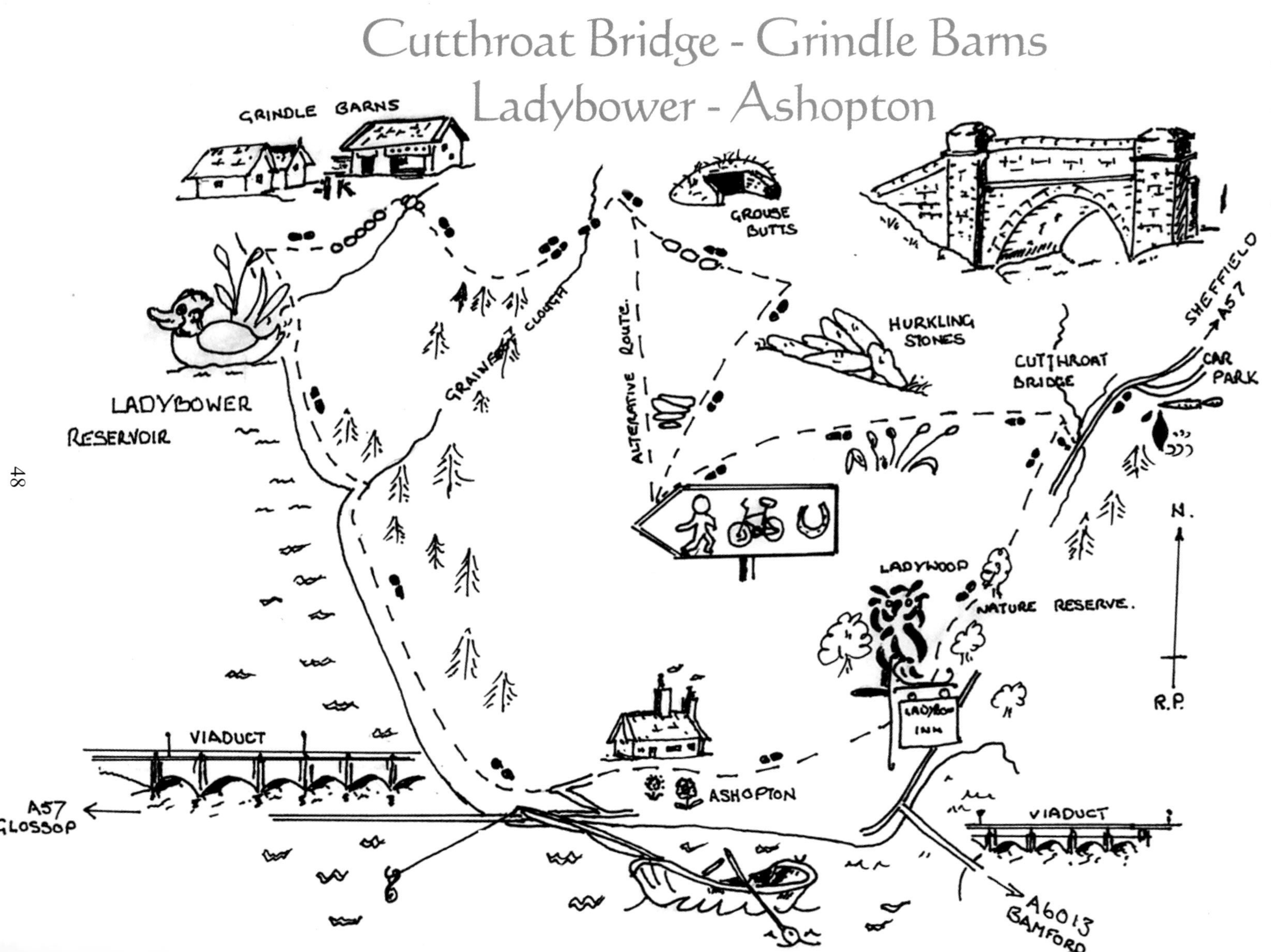

# Walk 8

# Cutthroat Bridge - Grindle Barns - Ladybower - Ashopton

## About this walk

If you are not familiar with this area, you are in for a real treat! One of our favourites, this one. Wonderful and dramatic views over the reservoirs and rolling peaks. The walk offers a huge contrast between moorland, woodland and 'reservoir side'. (The Ladybower Inn may beckon near the end.)

**Distance** 10km 6.2 miles

**Terrain** A moderate walk with just one longish but steady pull towards the end. An option is given to go up to Whinstone Lee Tor, for wonderful views. A mixture of footpaths, tracks, lanes and a short stretch of roadside. Generally sound underfoot.

**Map** OS Outdoor Leisure 1 The Peak District, Dark Peak area. 1:25 000 scale.

**Starting Point** Car park (large off-road lay-by). From Bamford go along A6013, cross Ladybower Reservoir and turn right at traffic lights, onto A57. Lay-by is one mile ahead on right.
Grid reference SK 216 874.

**Refreshments** The Ladybower Inn is close to the start (or finish) of the walk.

1. Exit at lower end of car park (reservoir side) and turn ***left*** to walk down side of road
2. Soon, on coming to bridge, cross road, go through small gate and continue up rocky path.

✓ **Cutthroat Bridge is said to be named after a gruesome murder around 400 years ago. Robert Ridge came across a man with a wound to his throat. The man was still alive, so Ridge and others carried him to a nearby house and then on to Bamford Hall where he died two days later. The victim had been found lying close to where a road bridge was later built. Remembering the murder, local people called it Cutthroat Bridge.**

3. Follow this path, as it winds uphill for some distance
4. Close to top of hill, as several paths meet, take _sharp_ right-hand path and head up to high rocks (**Whinstone Lee Tor**) _see note below_

❖ **The views from the top of this hill are truly stunning, but if you wish to avoid the climb, then instead of following instruction 4, take the next path and head down, with reservoir on your left. The paths link up 3/4 mile ahead (ignore stile and gateways approx. 1/4 mile along). Just past where path joins from right, go through single gate in wall on left and head down towards Derwent Reservoir. Then continue from instruction 9.**

5. Continue up for some distance, past low rock formation over on right (**Hurkling Rocks**)
6. Eventually, on coming to where paths cross (grouse butt on right), turn ***left*** and head down hill (towards **Derwent Reservoir**). This path descends gradually for some distance

✓ **The stone structures on your right are grouse butts, taken from the Gaelic word 'buta'. These are usually small stone, wood and turf constructions, used to give cover to the shooters. The birds are driven or flushed out of the heather towards the guns. Dogs are sometimes used to retrieve the birds.**

7. At end of path, on meeting 'T-junction' (wall ahead), turn ***right*** (wall now on left)
8. Shortly, go through gateway on left and head on down
9. Go through gate in corner of field and carry on down (wood on left)
10. Go through several gates and continue down, crossing small stream. Go through further gate, by barns

✓ **Grindle Barns have been restored by the National Trust to provide an information point and shelter.**

11. Go through small gate by large one and follow paved path down
12. At end of path, go through small gate, turn ***left***, go through further gate and walk along wide track (reservoir on right)

✓ **In 1935 the massive project of building the Ladybower Dam began, despite considerable controversy. Two lovely villages, Derwent and Ashopton, were lost beneath the waters of the reservoir, which was completed in 1943 but took a further two years to fill. The remains of Derwent village have been seen in some very dry summers such as 1959, 1976 and 1995. The spire of its church was left standing until 1947, when it was demolished. Most villagers were rehoused at Yorkshire Bridge, a few miles away.**

*Looking across to Ladybower*

*Ladybower Reservoir near the dam*

13. Continue along for some time, passing through a gate

14. Eventually, when road bridge is immediately on right and track starts to curve left, shortly go through small gate by large one

15. After gate, take lane bearing left up hill (ignore lane leading straight on to main road)

16. Go past houses and continue as lane becomes track (ignore gates on left going up into woods). Pass through a number of gates as track winds around hill for some time

✓ **The second set of buildings on your right is the back of the Ladybower Inn.**

17. Eventually, as path joins track, turn ***left*** up hill (towards **Cutthroat Bridge**)

❖ **If you wish to call into the Ladybower Inn, turn right at this point and walk down to road. Turn right for the Inn. Return to this point to continue walk.**

18. Go through gate (into **Ladybower Wood**) and continue up (ignore any paths off)

19. As track bears up to left, go straight on along track. Cross small stream and go through gate

20. Eventually, as path splits, take right-hand path down to bridge and road (visible just below). Cross road, turn ***left*** and walk back to car park

# Walk 9

## Ladybower Reservoir
## Yorkshire Bridge
## Win Hill

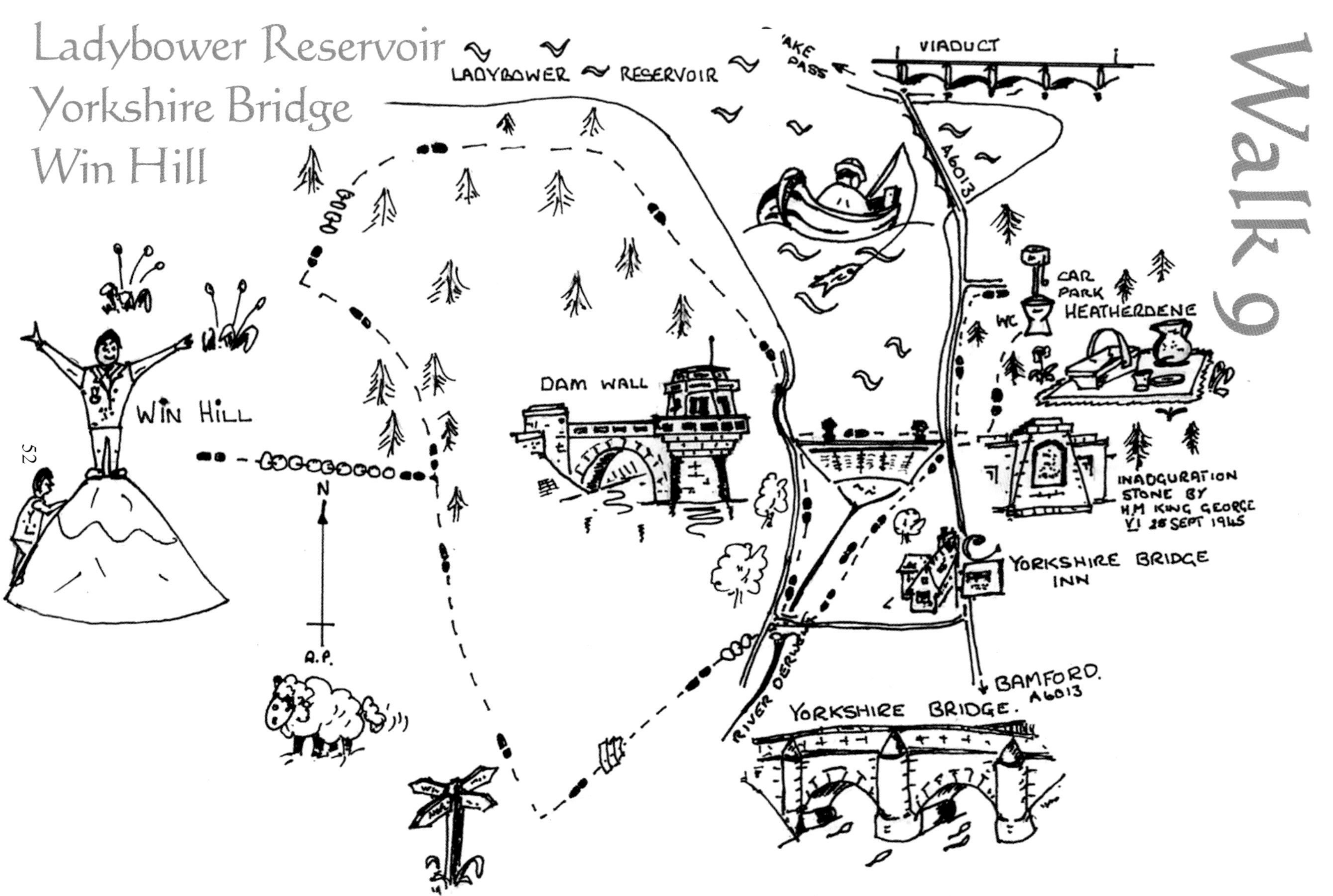

# Walk 9

# Ladybower Reservoir - Yorkshire Bridge - Win Hill

## About this walk

Perhaps the most stunning views of the reservoir walks! Worth taking the option of going to the top of Win Hill for breathtaking (particularly on a windy day!) panoramic views. An impressive walk taking in reservoir, woodland and a great contrast of scenery. A wide variety of flora to be found en route.

**Distance** 7.6km 4.7 miles

**Terrain** A gradual, steady climb soon after the start of the walk and a short, but steep climb up Win Hill, if you take that option. After that, mainly downhill or level with just a short pull up to the roadside. A mixture of roadside, footpaths, tracks and quiet road. Generally sound underfoot.

**Map** OS Outdoor Leisure 1 The Peak District, Dark Peak area. 1:25 000 scale.

**Starting Point** Heatherdene car park. From Bamford, along A6013. Just past Ladybower Dam (before bridge across reservoir), turn right into car park. Wonderful public toilets are also here!
Grid reference SK 202 859.

**Refreshments** No refreshments en route. Ladybower and Yorkshire Bridge Inns are both close by.

1. From car park entrance, cross road and turn ***left***. Walk beside road to dam (**Ladybower Reservoir** on right)
2. By 2nd set of large gates, take path down into valley (ignore pavement going straight on and do not cross dam)

✓ **In 1935 the massive project of building the Ladybower Dam began, despite considerable controversy. Two lovely villages, Derwent and Ashopton, were lost beneath the waters of the reservoir, which was completed in 1943 but took a further two years to fill. The remains of Derwent village have been seen in some very dry summers such as 1959, 1976 and 1995. The spire of its church was left standing until 1947, when it was demolished. The villagers were re-housed at Yorkshire Bridge, a few miles away.**

3. Cross tiny stone bridge and carry on along path
4. As path meets track, turn ***left*** and continue. Just before large gate leading to road, bear right and follow path
5. Very shortly, go through single gate, turn ***right*** and go over **Yorkshire Bridge** (crossing **River Derwent**). Follow road round to left
6. Very soon (just past gateway), turn ***right*** up a few steps and follow path up hill. Go through gate and continue up
7. On meeting wide track, turn ***left*** and almost immediately ***right***. Continue on up

✓ **The track you have just crossed was a railway line built between 1901 and 1903 to carry thousands of tons of stone needed for the construction of Howden and Derwent dams. This came from Bole Hill quarry, Grindleford.**

8. Go through gap in wall and bear slightly right across field towards opposite wall

✓ **Bamford village can be seen ahead in the distance. The name derives from the early English 'Beam-ford', which literally means 'wooden footbridge'. The 'ford-with-a-beam' lay on an ancient trade-route which led northwards from the Hope Valley and across the moors into Yorkshire.**

9. Go through stile or gap in wall, bear slightly right and head for opposite wall

10. Go through gap, bear right, cross small stream and follow path up

11. Eventually, as path meets another, turn ***right*** and head up towards **Win Hill** (ignore paths straight on and to left)

12. Go through large gate and continue up. Pass through single gate and follow path as it curves left (wall on left)

13. Very soon, as path joins wide track, turn ***right*** and continue up this track. Keep to track (ignore paths off)

14. As track levels out, continue for some time (wall on left)

✓ **To the right can be seen the hamlet of Yorkshire Bridge and Ladybower Reservoir. The hamlet is named after an ancient bridge. This was crossed by Jaggers (men who led teams of pack horses) and was the last bridge before the Yorkshire border. In 1695 the wooden bridge was replaced by a stone one, better able to bear the weight of the pack-horse teams.**

15. Near wood, where path appears to split, take right-hand lower path and continue on (wall on left) into **Ladybower Wood** (ignore small gate on right to Yorkshire Bridge)

❖ **The path going up to left (just inside wood) is a concessionary one (landowners have the right to withdraw the use of it) to top of Win Hill. The spectacular, panoramic views from Win Hill are well worth the effort. If you wish to go up there, return afterwards to this point and continue from instruction 16.**

16. Continue on through wood. Eventually, at edge of wood, go through gate or over stile and turn ***right***

❖ **For an alternative (right of way) path to Win Hill, turn left here and follow path up. At brow of hill, turn right and continue up to summit. Then return afterwards to this point and continue from instruction 17.**

17. Go down hill, keeping to edge of wood. Very soon, bear left and follow path to wall opposite (wall on right)

18. Shortly, turn ***right*** and go through gate in right-hand boundary

19. Continue straight on down through trees to further gate opposite. Continue down, passing through several more gates

Looking down towards Bamford

20. Follow track as it winds down hill (ignore paths off). Towards bottom of hill, on reaching a wide track (T-junction), turn ***right*** (ignore path going down a few steps almost opposite). Walk up track

21. In a while, cross small stream and a little further on, go through small gate by large one

22. Almost immediately, cross wide track and continue straight on (keep reservoir on left)

23. On meeting another wide track, turn ***right*** and then immediately ***left.*** Go through small gate. Continue down path to **Ladybower Reservoir**

24. At reservoir, turn ***right*** and walk along lane

- **The way across the dam is usually open to the public. This can be used as a short cut back to the car park if desired. It rejoins walk at instruction 28.**

25. Continue for some distance and then go through small gate by large one, leading to **Yorkshire Bridge**. On reaching road, turn ***left*** and cross bridge

26. Almost immediately, turn ***left*** through small gate. Follow path and shortly turn ***left*** to walk along wide track

27. Just before large gate, turn ***right*** and follow path for some time to **Ladybower Dam**

28. Follow path up to meet road. At road, turn ***left*** and follow road back to car park on right (reservoir on left)

- **If you prefer, take a more pleasant route back to car park (which is the same distance) by crossing road and going up steps by memorial. At top of steps, turn left and follow path to car park.**

# The Chatsworth Walks

*Last remaining cottage of the old Edensor village*

*Rutland Arms, Baslow*

*Peacock Inn*

*Baslow Church clock*

# Sarah's Tale

Joseph has always said that he knew he wanted us to be married within half an hour of setting eyes on me. And I think it was true. I can still see him clearly, sitting at the servants' table in that huge kitchen, scoffing eggs and ham and oatcakes, with cup after cup of tea. Such an appetite, if appearing slightly gross on that occasion, was certainly forgivable. He had, we were soon to be informed, travelled overnight from London, by comet coach to Chesterfield, then walked over the darkened and bleak moors, to reach Chatsworth at around four o'clock in the morning. After scaling a gate, (how I loved the thought of that!) he had made a private tour of discovery around the grounds. His Grace the Duke was absent, having just left for Russia, where he was to be a guest at the Coronation of Emperor Nicholas. Joseph had made sure that the gardeners started work early - by six o'clock - and with clear instructions regarding what was to be done. They must have realised, with something of a jolt, how life was going to change from that day onwards! But even in the raw chill of that spring morning, I suspect they drank in the enthusiasm of this twenty-three year-old newcomer, and were won over by his sociable manner. Impossible not to be, as I myself had found, within minutes of his acquaintance. As the Duke, only a short time before, had also very quickly discovered.

I felt such an energy about the man that I found I could barely touch my own - much lighter - breakfast. Quite impossible not be transfixed by him, and of course the instant connection between us was noticed quickly enough by my aunt, the housekeeper. In between presenting him with platefuls of hearty fare, she sat with us, sipping a cup of tea, and taking him in with a fascination almost equal to mine.

He got his wish, of course. We were married in Edensor some nine months later, 20th of February 1827, and moved into a pleasantly substantial cottage, to the edge of the kitchen garden. I put my slight anxiety, about being three and a half years his senior, to one side. I had never had reason to consider myself pretty, and had never, until then, received a proposal. But I was trimly enough built, not altogether plain, and educated to a reasonable level. Moreover, thanks to my father's success as a small mill owner, I had a fortune of five thousand pounds to put our disposal. Joseph came with nothing whatever, but of course was now one of the highest paid people of the estate. Not that money was ever an influence with him in this matter, I am quite sure not. I know my husband feels a huge affection for me and he has expressed this, over the years, often and quite ardently. Nor, despite so many long absences, have I ever felt anything but total trust in him. The children and I have one rival only for his time and his attention - the Duke. And in this contest, William Cavendish, sixth Duke of Devonshire, has always been the undisputed winner.

Being the loser is particularly hard for me to accept at the present time. The baby is due within two or three weeks, and I feel heavy and weary beyond measure, more so than with any of the others. Joseph will not be at home when it is born, that is quite certain. He left only days ago to join the Duke in Geneva, and there is no reason to suppose that this will be a short trip. My aunt has heard (and she hears of most things) that the Duke has it in mind to travel as far as Constantinople, and not via a direct route, but probably dawdling in Italy for a long period. No doubt Joseph will see many wonderful things, as he always does, and bring back many rare and precious plants for the gardens, as is always the case. And the Duke himself will enjoy the adventure so very much more in Joseph's company, of that there is no doubt. My husband can always raise the master's spirits or calm his anxieties, always share his enthusiasm for extravagant purchases to improve the House or - far more important to Joseph - its grounds. They have a most remarkable friendship. A close bond between two men of vastly different backgrounds, however talented a person my husband is said to be - and no one is more proud of his skills than I am. So I can only accept and wonder at his present situation - the Duke's right-hand man and true soul mate. I do my best to be patient and to bear up in the background of it all, though at times, as now, that is far from easy. But certainly I have no difficulty in remaining busy, caring for our three girls and for little George, while keeping an eye on Joseph's projects within the estate.

George is quite a handful, and I've no doubt it's because we all spoil him. Hard not to, when he was born barely a year after our first son died, that wretched December of 1835. William was a month short of his sixth birthday, measles was about in the village, and no remedies relieved his violent coughing or brightened that terrible pallor. Joseph managed to be home, thank God, though he had made it only by a few days. He was heartbroken, we all were. What greater loss is there, than the loss of a child? But of course, his life kept him very busy and the Duke, as always, was most kind.

If His Grace were married, with children of his own, then perhaps his demands on Joseph would be less onerous, who can say? But he is not, unusual though that situation is for a man in his position. Heaven knows, he would have no difficulty in finding a suitable match, even now, at the age of forty-eight. Duke William is not unattractive, though he's put on a fair amount of weight in recent years and is also becoming increasingly deaf. But he's highly sociable and popular, quite 'undukelike' at times, more a man of the people. When ordinary folk arrive at the House entrance, asking to be shown around - and that can happen on any day - he will often do this job himself, if he is not busy. People do not always realise they are with His Grace, and not a servant - or only when he refuses any payment, at the end of their visit.

There's certainly no shortage of parties and entertaining at Chatsworth, even though the Duke has calmed down a bit, since his youth. My aunt, Mrs Gregory, has often told me how it was when he first came into the title, at just twenty one years of age. His parties were truly legendary then, and not only at Chatsworth. He owns Hardwick Hall, as well as Bolton Abbey up in Yorkshire and Devonshire House in London, amongst others. Whole groups of servants regularly have to move from one property to another. The man must be the most eligible bachelor in England, but he has never succumbed to any pressure. Apparently he is quite content to know that he will be succeeded by a cousin, another William Cavendish, who is married to the Duke's niece, Blanche. His Grace truly adores Blanche. Only she, aside from Joseph, has his total trust. And she has already produced a healthy son, so he is relieved of all concerns.

Not that he is without interest in women, you understand. Until last year, there had been a quite intense relationship - it must have carried on for around ten years. Joseph knew of it and so did a handful of others, but from most it was kept a well-guarded secret. Eliza Warwick, that's her name. He used to see her in London, mainly, though she did stay a night or two at Chatsworth at one stage. That caused no stir, of course, because the place has always had an endless stream of guests. At one point he got her installed in the Rookery, in Ashford-in-the-Water. Apparently she hated the place. Couldn't stand the countryside - especially when the Duke was away, which of course he very often was. And even when he was home, she was certainly not part of his entertaining. You can be quite sure she was nowhere to be seen when Princess Victoria and her mother came to stay, a few years back! So poor Eliza couldn't wait to get back to the city and her social circle. I can sympathise with the loneliness, of course, because it's something I've had to put up with in almost equal measure. But at least I'm the wife of a good and talented man, and one who is faithful to me, which the Duke almost certainly was not to Eliz, as he called her, despite her long hold on him.

Joseph heard that Eliz suffered two miscarriages during their early days, though whether those were accidents of nature or not is another thing. She was obviously not of appropriate status for the Duke to marry, or it may be that he would have done so. But perhaps it needs to be said about the Duke that, despite his lovers, and his great sociability, he leads a far more restrained life than did his mother. She, of course, was Duchess Georgiana, wife of the fifth Duke. Georgiana gave birth to children not fathered by her husband, and she, in her turn, was happy to tolerate his infidelity. Her closest friend was a mistress of the Duke, and the mother of two of his children. A very strange arrangement - better tolerated in those days, no doubt, than it would be now. But Georgiana was a great public figure also, because she got herself much involved in the politics of the day - hosting meetings and social events to support the Whig party. Even took to leading marches along the streets of London, handing out pamphlets, chatting and joking with shopkeepers and the like. Quite incredible, for a Duchess.

Her son is much less interested in politics, and he loves Chatsworth far more than either of his parents did. They spent most of their time in the London property, so I understand. Our own Duke does have some political responsibilities, naturally. The King places great reliance on his advice, and would love to bind him in further. But Duke William is enthralled by this place, it is his true home. That is why he brought Joseph here, of course. The two of them had previously, on a number of occasions, talked together in the grounds of the Duke's property in Chiswick: it so happened that part of this land was leased to the Horticultural Society, which employed Joseph at the time. Their conversations were enough to convince him that the young gardener should be given his chance. A chance to make the grounds of Chatsworth beautiful and unique.

Georgiana and the fifth Duke saw this place merely as a country retreat, somewhere to invite their 'London crowd' to. They had left both the House and the gardens very neglected. His Grace has certainly changed all that. He's added a whole new north wing. The interior has been completely rearranged, decorators and craftsmen are often at work, and he is rapidly filling the place with sculptures, paintings, ornaments, dining services and heaven knows what else, mostly gathered from his trips abroad. It is all becoming a little too ornate in there, for my taste, I am more drawn towards a plainer look. But certainly no one could accuse him of neglect.

And, of course - the gardens. Joseph has completely redesigned them and they boast trees, plants and flowers from much of the globe. The Chatsworth Gardens are now famous and the name of Joseph Paxton has become more and more known, along with them. His advice is sought increasingly from the aristocratic and the very rich. There's little doubt that many would pay well to win his unshared services, but the Duke treasures his friend far too greatly. And Duke William is generous enough to us. It is some years now since we moved from our first cottage into a far more substantial property.

Joseph has designed a colossal glass construction and it is now taking shape behind the House - the Great Conservatory, as people are naming it. He asked me, before his departure, to keep an eye on progress and to inform him about any problems. We write to each other frequently, but letters take at least two weeks to arrive and often he has moved on before they do. He is wildly excited by this new building. It will be the biggest of its kind anywhere in the world. The Duke's guests will be able to drive a horse and carriage through the middle of it with ease, and to view in there a wonder of flowers and plants, that can thrive only in the climate its eight huge boilers and seven miles of iron pipe will create. Plants they will bring home in great quantities from this trip, I've no doubt.

Joseph is also helping the Duke with his plans for Edensor village to be completely rebuilt. The place has never been anything to boast about, that's to be sure. It's a ragged collection of poky cottages, all of them rather unsanitary and evil smelling, and they really are quite an eyesore when you look across from the front of the House. I've heard it suggested that the Duke is interested only in being rid of such a view, but Joseph is certainly not of that opinion. Duke William has always taken a great interest in the welfare of his estate workers, hugely more so than any before him. This new Edensor is to be built just out of view at the far side of the road, instead of straddling the two sides, as it does at present, and it will be so much better. A great deal of time has been spent on its design, and every house is to have running water and proper sanitation. The villagers - who have heard something of the plans - are looking forward to the move, and not a little grateful.

I'm sure I must have talked for long enough. If you should choose to visit this great House (and surely you must, at some point in your life?) - then you will see, as you wander around its grounds, the wonders created by Joseph, with remarkably little change since. But sadly, his great conservatory has now gone. The Duke's successors were not to enjoy his wealth, and in the end it became far too expensive to heat. With considerable difficulty - even with the help of explosives - it was finally destroyed in 1923. But that extraordinary glass building was the inspiration for what later proved to be Joseph's greatest achievement of all - the building of the Crystal Palace in London. This would persuade Queen Victoria to give him the title of 'Sir' (and his wife that of 'Lady', though it never sat comfortably with me), and would make the name Paxton a famous one. But inevitably, it took him from my side ever more.

My husband remained a loyal servant of the Duke, until His Grace's death in the New Year of 1858. Joseph died seven years later, a successful and much admired man. He is buried in the churchyard of the new Edensor, as am I. My memory lies quietly in the shadow of his, as completely as my life once did.

# Historical Note

The career of Joseph Paxton is a real 'rags to riches' story. He was born in Bedfordshire in 1803, the seventh son of a rather poor farming family. Around the age of 15, he found work as a garden boy and a few years later was taken on by the Horticultural Society. Through this, he had the good fortune to meet the Duke of Devonshire, who offered him the position of head gardener at Chatsworth, at the age of just twenty three.

Paxton turned out to be immensely creative and skilled, but just as importantly he became a close friend and frequent travelling companion of the Duke. He remained head gardener at Chatsworth until the Duke's death in 1858, but took on an immense number of other projects, including the design for many public parks. He was knighted by Queen Victoria in October 1851, following his successful design of the Crystal Palace in London. Paxton became very wealthy, through investing in the railways. He was elected Liberal MP for Coventry in 1854, and held this position until he died in 1865.

This tale is told by Joseph Paxton's rather long suffering wife, and all the people and circumstances she describes are real. Sarah had to bear much family responsibility during her husband's frequent and long absences, always accepting where his first duty lay. She does not appear to have sought any limelight herself, feeling more comfortable in the background, and she always remained at their house on the Chatsworth estate. Sarah outlived her husband by six years, and both are now buried in Edensor churchyard.

*Chatsworth House*

# Walk 10

## Calton Lees (car park)
## Rowsley
## Beeley

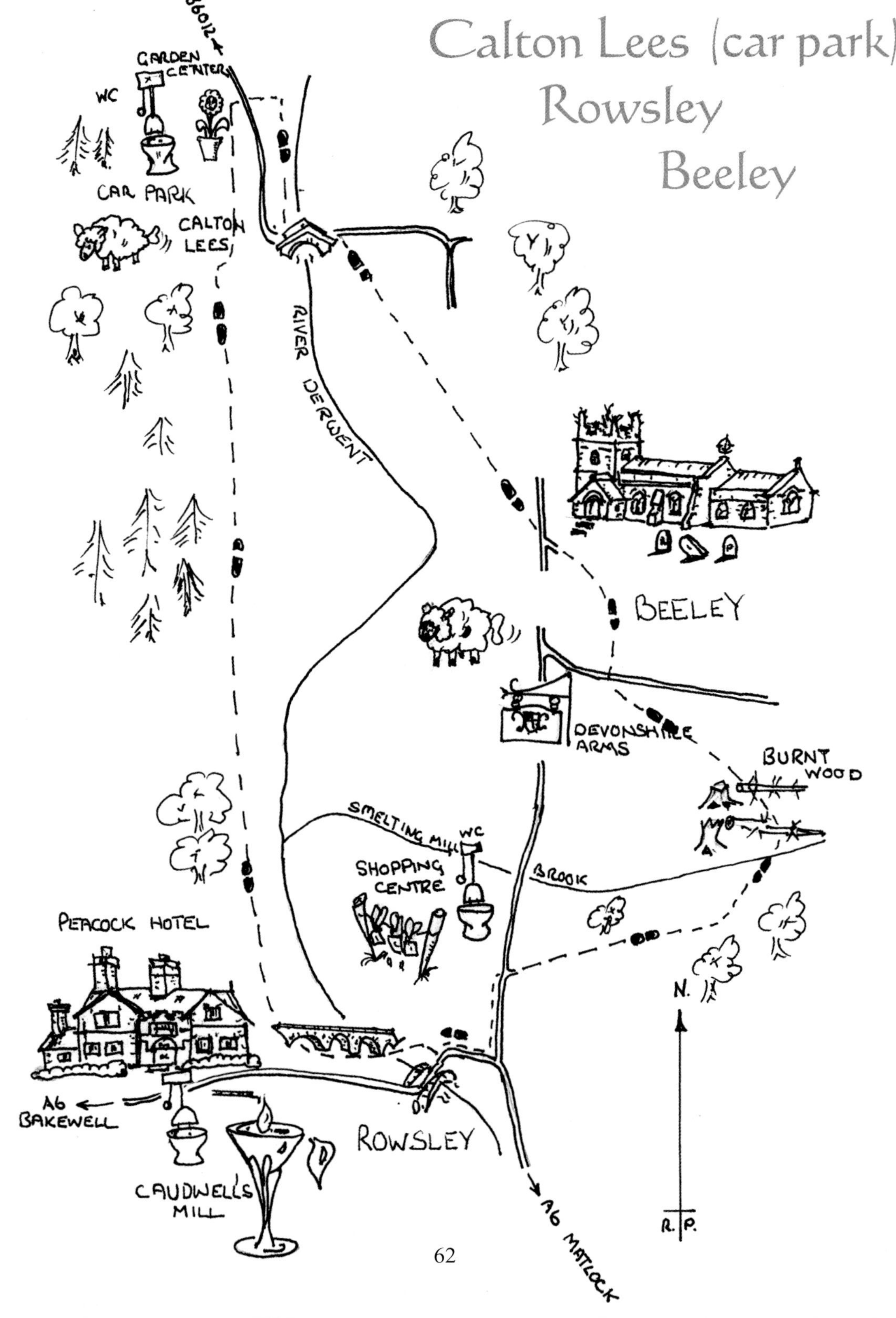

# Walk 10

# Calton Lees (car park) - Rowsley - Beeley

## About this walk

An attractive walk across part of the Chatsworth estate and through the villages of Rowsley and Beeley. The route embraces parkland, riverside and woodland with views over the rolling hills. Why not take a break at the interesting Caudwell's water driven flour mill, with the craftshop, workshops and café?

**Distance** 8km 5 miles

**Terrain** A fairly undemanding walk with a slight rise from Rowsley up through Rowsley Wood. A mixture of footpaths, tracks, pavement. Generally good underfoot.

**Map** OS Explorer OL24 The Peak District, White Peak area. 1:25 000 scale.

**Starting Point** Calton Lees car park, just off B6012, far end of Chatsworth Park from direction of Sheffield. Grid reference SK 258 685.

**Refreshments** Garden centre café and toilets at beginning of walk. Café/restaurant at Caudwell's Mill and pub restaurants in Rowsley.

1. From car park, walk short distance down to road and turn ***right*** (away from entrance and towards garden centre)
2. Walk along road for some distance (ignore left off to garden centre)
3. Continue along road as it turns sharp left, just past houses (ignore track straight on and to right)
4. Carry on up past houses, and as road turns right, go over stile by gate ahead
5. Turn ***left*** and follow path (wall on left). Near bottom left-hand corner of field, go over stile (by gateway) in left-hand wall
6. With back to stile, turn ***right*** and walk down (wall on right). Almost immediately, bear very slightly diagonally left to curve of wall ahead
7. Pass through gateway and walk straight on towards wall and trees in distance ahead. Go through gateway in wall and straight on
8. Continue along path as it bears left (river on left, wood on right)
9. Go over stile (in gateway) in right-hand wall near end of field. Follow path straight on into trees
10. Shortly, go over stile by gateway and continue as path curves right (wall on right). As wall ends, continue on as path curves right and becomes a wide track
11. Follow wide track for some distance (river on left), passing through several gateways
12. Eventually, track meets road (just after passing under old railway bridge). Turn ***left*** and follow **Church Lane** into **Rowsley village**, past side of **Peacock Inn**
13. On meeting main road A6(T) turn ***left***

❖ **You may wish to visit the attractive Caudwell's Mill, with its water powered flour mill. It has an excellent café offering snacks and meals and also various craft shops. Turn right, cross over road and follow signs. Come back to this point and continue.**

14. Follow road over bridge and walk along side of road as it bears right

15. As road bears sharply right (towards **Matlock**), turn ***left*** towards **Chatsworth** and follow pavement

16. Carry straight on (past entrance to **Peak Village Outlets**)

✓ **Peak village offers a variety of shops and has a café.**

17. By house numbers 23 and 24, cross road and head up track opposite (at time of writing, next to **Country Store**)

18. Continue up track for some distance and as it becomes a path, carry on into woodland

✓ **Worth getting your breath back here, looking at lovely wide views behind.**

19. On meeting path ahead (T-junction), turn ***left*** and head down hill (ignore right, leading to wide upper path)

20. Follow path down as it curves right (ignore path going left). Follow path as it winds down and then up through woods for some distance (ignore paths off)

*St. Anne's Church, Beeley*

21. Eventually, cross footbridge and after a few steps turn ***right*** up hill. Go through gate and continue up hill (wall on left)

22. Soon, just past gate (in wall), go over stile in left-hand wall (farm over on right)

23. With back to wall, walk across field to wood and wall opposite

24. Cross stile (slightly to left) in wall, go down bank, turn ***right*** and follow path down through woods

25. At end of trees, go through stile and walk to stile in wall opposite (a little to left of gateway)

26. Go through this stile and head diagonally left (keeping wall on left as it meanders) to narrow stile in left-hand wall

27. Pass through this narrow stile and walk straight down right-hand side of field (**Beeley village** in distance)

✓ **The parish register shows Beeley village dates back to 1538. It was once part of the Chatsworth Estate, but now some houses are privately owned. The church of St. Anne was restored in the 19th century, although it dates back to Norman times. At weddings, tradition demands that the bride and groom must not approach by the west gate and must pay coinage to leave by the narrow east gate. The wider one is used for funerals. A bride died, on her way to be married, in 1785 (wonder which gate she used?).**

28. At bottom right-hand corner of field, turn ***right*** through gateway. Go straight on (fence on left) and go through small gate in left-hand corner

29. Cross road and go through another small gate. Go slightly right across field to trees opposite

30. Pass through line of trees (past stone posts) and follow path as it heads down diagonally right and then left

31. On meeting wall at bottom of hill, go through gated stile in this wall

32. Cross footbridge and continue up lane (ignore lane to left). On meeting another lane, turn *left*. Follow this lane past **Duke's Barn** (on right)

✓ **Duke's Barn, built in 1791, once housed the cart horses used in transport for the Chatsworth Estate. It is now a residential outdoor centre.**

33. Follow road as it bears right (ignore road to left). Turn ***left*** down by church

34. On meeting road, cross over (care needed here, as road can be busy) and go through stile and gate

35. With back to stile, turn ***right*** and follow path. Continue on path as it bears diagonally left to top left-hand corner of field

36. Go through gate by bridge. Cross road, turn ***left*** and go over bridge

37. Almost immediately, turn ***right*** through gate and walk straight on (river on right)

38. Just in front of ruin of old mill, turn ***left*** up to road. Cross road, turn ***left***, back to car park

# Walk II

Calton Lees
Swiss Cottage
Chatsworth House

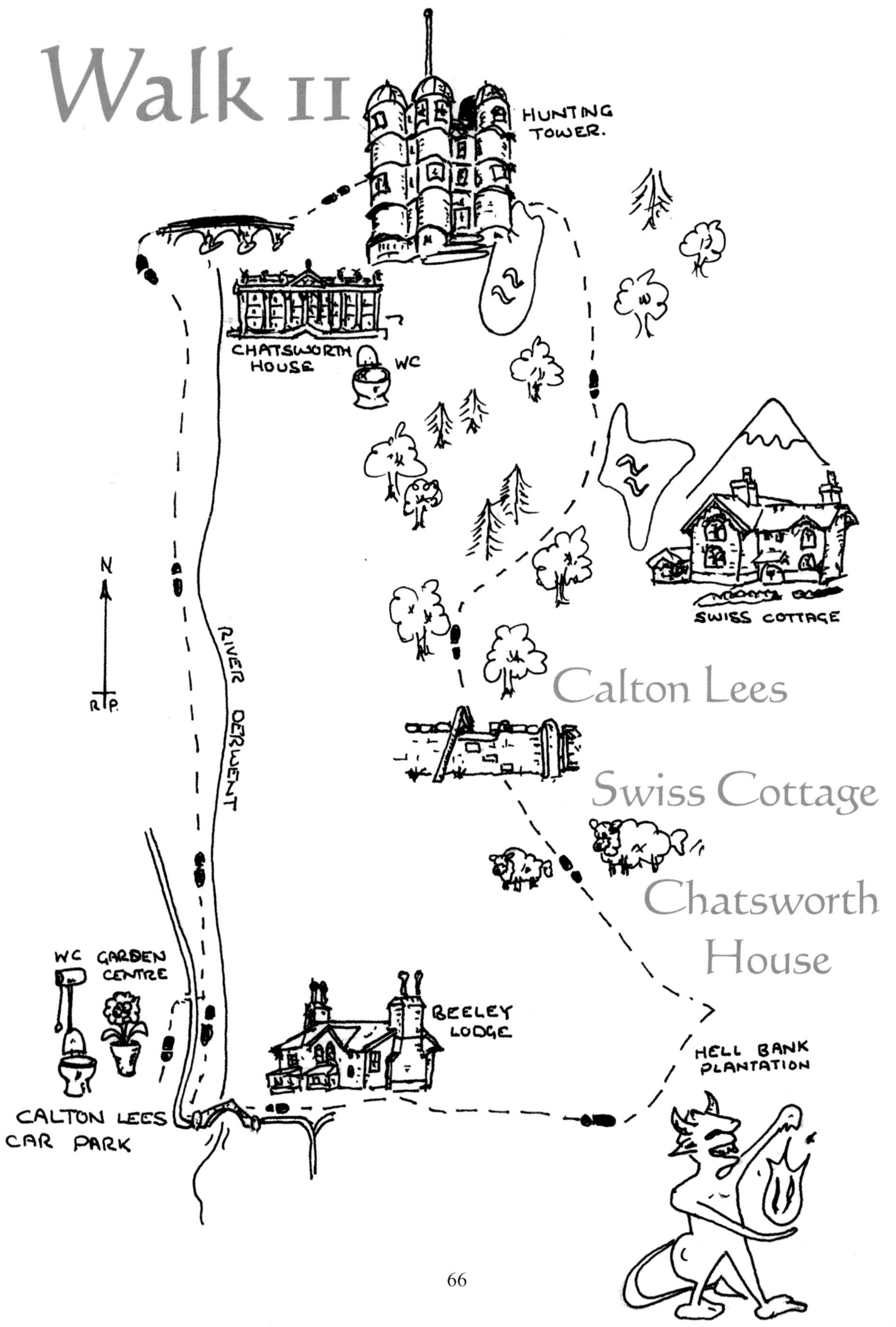

# Walk 11

# Calton Lees - Swiss Cottage - Chatsworth House

## About this walk

This is a most attractive walk and also a relatively undemanding one. It keeps entirely within the impressive Chatsworth Estate, taking in some of its less well known landmarks and guiding you past the House itself. The walk encompasses a variety of countryside, including woodland, riverside, lakeside, parkland and beautiful views across the Chatsworth Estate. Parts of the middle section of the walk are along Chatsworth paths, open to the public by kind permission of the Estate.

**Distance** 10km 6.2 miles

**Terrain** A fairly undemanding route with a gradual ascent during the early part of the walk, but after this mainly flat or downhill. Approaching House from Hunting Tower, a choice is given between descending steps or keeping to the lane. A mixture of fairly even footpaths, tracks and roadway.

**Map** OS Explorer OL24 The Peak District, White Peak area. 1:25 000 scale.

**Starting Point** Calton Lees car park, just off B6012, far end of Chatsworth Park from direction of Sheffield. Grid reference SK 258 685.

**Refreshments** Garden centre café and toilets at beginning of walk. Refreshments, café, shop and toilets available at Chatsworth House, towards end of walk.

1. Walk back to far side of car park (Chatsworth House end). Go through gate and cross road (by cattle grid)
2. Go down steps and carry on to riverside (old mill on left). Turn ***right*** and follow path to bridge (river on left)
3. Go through gate and turn ***left***. Cross over bridge and walk alongside road
4. Carry straight on and just as road curves right, turn ***left*** (ignore entrance to house)
5. Follow lane up for some distance (passing buildings and farm on right - ignore stile on left). Keep going up lane (ignore paths off to right and left)
6. Eventually, as lane curves sharp right, go over stile in wall (on left) by large gate
7. Go straight on and follow wide track as it winds up hill (heading back on yourself)
8. Keep on track (as beautiful views of the valley and **Chatsworth Estate** open up on left) for some distance
9. Eventually, as track meets wood (farm over to right in distance) go over stile by large gate. Follow track straight on into woods and over small stream
10. At crossroads, continue straight on (ignore lanes going to right and left)
11. Continue on lane for some time (ignore track on right leading to **Swiss Cottage**)
12. Continue past **Swiss Lake** (**Swiss Cottage** on opposite side)

✓ **Swiss Lake feeds the Cascade, which can be seen when visiting Chatsworth House gardens. This striking waterfall was built around 1700 for the 4th Duke. The Cascade drops over 200 yards down the hill, in a fall of 24 steps.**

13. Carry on past **Emperor Lake** (ignore tracks off to right and left)

✓ **Emperor Lake was built by the 6th Duke to provide the water for the Emperor fountain, which can rise to a height of 300 feet in front of the House. The lake is home to many wildfowl, especially geese, swans and coots.**

14. As lane curves left and goes down hill, continue on (ignore lanes to right and left)

15. Carry on down lane as it winds past **Hunting Tower**

✓ **The Hunting Tower offers spectacular views and seats just up steps on left. Built by Bess of Hardwick, it was originally known as Stand Tower. She is believed to have used the small, turreted tower to view hunting in the Park.**

16. Almost immediately after steps up to Hunting Tower, as lane curves left, turn ***right*** and take path and then steps down

❖ **If you prefer an alternative to steps (easier but longer), follow lane round. Rejoin walk at farmyard (instruction 19).**

*Old Mill, Chatsworth Park*

*Queen Mary's Bower was named after Mary, Queen of Scots, who was brought to Chatsworth as a prisoner of the Earl of Shrewsbury (Bess of Hardwick's fourth husband). It is believed she was allowed to take the 'ayre' in this moated building by the river.*

17. Continue on as path winds down and meets lane. Cross over lane and continue down
18. On meeting lane, turn ***right*** and walk down hill
19. Walk past large gate on right (leads to farmyard) and continue down. Go through gate by cattle grid and continue down through car park (past restaurant buildings and House)

✓ **Toilets, refreshments, café and information available at Chatsworth House.**

20. Carry on down past House and at end of wall, cross over access road and continue down towards river and bridge
21. Go through gate and across bridge. Immediately, turn ***left*** and follow path (river and House on left) for some distance
22. Eventually, on meeting old ruined mill, turn ***right*** and walk up to road. Cross road and turn ***left*** back to car park

# Walk 12

## Baslow Bubnell The Edges

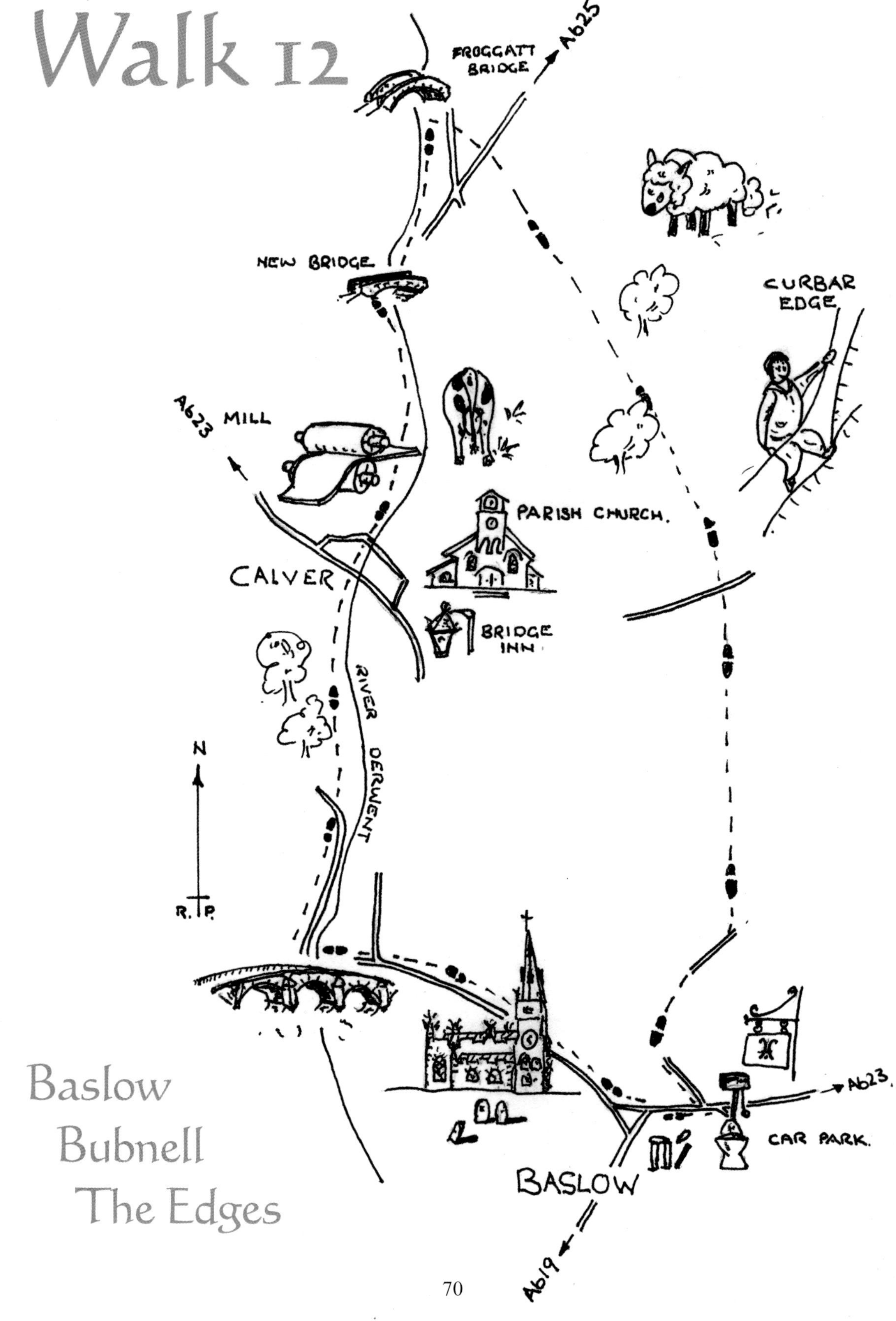

# Walk 12

## Baslow - Bubnell - The Edges

### About this walk

This is a beautiful walk along the side of the River Derwent and below the edges of Froggatt, Curbar and Baslow. It offers a wide variety of scenery and extensive views over the rolling hills and countryside. Best enjoyed on a clear day to appreciate the stunning outlook.

**Distance** 10.4km 6.4 miles

**Terrain** Not a difficult walk, but parts of the route can be very muddy after heavy rain. Best walked during drier periods. A mixture of footpaths, tracks, riversides, meadows and quiet roads.

**Map** OS Explorer OL24 The Peak District, White Peak area. 1:25 000 scale.

**Starting Point** Car park in Baslow, off A619 (from direction of Chesterfield). On left by village green and before Cavendish Hotel. Public toilets by car park. Grid reference SK 258 721.

**Refreshments** Baslow has a number of pubs and restaurants. There is also a café and a small number of village shops.

1. From car park, walk back to entrance and turn ***left***. Walk along road, passing **Cavendish Hotel**
2. Just past entrance to **Baslow Sports Fields**, cross road (pelican crossing), turn ***left*** and continue into village
3. Continue past cemetery and shops. At church entrance, cross road and turn ***right***

✓ **St. Anne's is a lovely church and its tower, spire and doorway date back to the 14th century. Inside the porch is a Saxon coffin-lid, carved with two keys. On one face of the tower is the Victoria clock. This has the legend VICTORIA 1897, instead of numbers, and was made to commemorate the Diamond Jubilee of Queen Victoria. Near the door inside is a glass case containing a dog whip. In the 17th and 18th centuries this was used by the official 'dog whipper' to drive stray dogs out of the church. Some claim that it was also used to maintain order among worshippers and to wake up those who snored during the service!**

4. After a few paces, turn ***left***, cross bridge

✓ **This is an early 17th century, three arched bridge, which still has a little stone shelter built for the toll collector. The shelter is known locally as 'Mary Brady's House', after a local beggar who slept rough in it years ago. This is the only bridge across the Derwent never to have been destroyed by floods.**

5. From bridge, turn ***right*** and walk along lane (**Bubnell Lane**) for some distance, passing houses on left and **River Derwent** on right (ignore any ways off)

*Mary Brady's House*

6. Just before lane turns sharp left, go through stile on right. With back to stile, turn ***left***, walk a few paces towards gateway and then head diagonally right (keeping gateway on left) to stile in right-hand side of wall and fence opposite
7. Go through stile and head diagonally right. Follow path (wall on right now), then go through small gate by large one

✓ **Baslow and Curbar Edges are over on your right, in the distance.**

8. Continue along path, passing through edge of woods, old stile by stone gate posts and shortly beside river
9. Eventually, go through stile and continue straight on (river on right)
10. Pass through another stile and follow path to houses (keep close to river, ignore other paths). Go through small gate, over footbridge and follow path
11. Pass under bridge and up to road. Cross road, turn ***left*** and very shortly turn ***right***
12. Follow lane past entrance to **Calver Mill**, through gateway into **Stocking Farm**

✓ **Calver Mill was rebuilt in 1805 to replace an earlier mill destroyed by fire. It was a thriving cotton mill and employed many local people. It finished producing cotton in 1923. The building was used as Colditz Castle in the television series, Colditz. It has now been developed into luxury flats.**

13. Walk past right-hand side of farm buildings and through small gate by large one

14. Follow path slightly diagonally right to top right-hand side of field. Continue on (river on right)

15. Soon, go over stile by gate and continue along path

16. On meeting houses and road, turn ***right***, go over bridge and immediately cross road. Go down steps and turn ***right***

17. Follow path by river and eventually, on meeting road (in hamlet of **Froggatt**), go over stile in wall, turn ***right*** and walk up road

✓ **Froggatt Bridge dates from the 17th century and is unusual in having a large, pointed arch on the village side and a smaller one on the other. This is likely to be because the bridge was extended following the widening of the Derwent, when it was dammed at Calver.**

18. Soon, as road bears sharp right, cross road and go through stile and gate by large gates

19. Follow path up hill (houses on left). Continue up path, bearing right, to road. Go over stile in wall and turn ***right***

20. Walk down side of road (great care needed) and, as road bears right, just before houses, cross road

21. Go through gap in fence by large gate. With back to gate, follow path straight on (walls on left and right, soon on right only)

22. Continue on through woods (passing large house on right). Go over stile by large gate. Follow path through wood as it winds up

23. Soon, follow path as it bears sharply right (ignore path going straight on). Continue on for some considerable time. (**Froggatt** and **Curbar Edges** are up on your left)

24. Eventually, go through gate by large one. With back to gate, turn ***left*** and walk up hill (wall on left)

25. Go through gap in wall and gradually bear diagonally right over rocky area, to top right-hand corner

26. Go through stile in wall ahead. Head diagonally right to wall opposite and pass through small gate by large one. Turn ***right*** and walk down road

27. Just after road starts to curve right, and before **Curbar village**, cross road and go through stile on left (heading back on yourself). Follow path up (wall on right)

28. Go through stile and gate. With back to gate, take path heading diagonally right (ignore path going straight on) and follow path as it curves right again

29. Go through gate in wall opposite and follow path straight on (**Baslow Edge** on left). (Several paths are visible in this section of walk. Try to keep to main path, but they all join up eventually)

30. After a while, pass through gateway in wall and carry straight on

31. Approximately 100 metres before next wall ahead (wide gateway and stile visible), turn ***left*** up track (another path joins you from sharp right at this point)

32. Follow track as it winds up towards **Baslow Edge**. Eventually, on meeting wide, stony track, turn ***right*** and follow it down

❖ **If you would like to walk up to Wellington's Monument and the wonderful wide views from there, turn left instead of right and walk up track. Then return to this point and continue down track.**

✓ **For those following the above detour:**
**Wellington's Monument was erected in 1866, probably in honour of the Duke of Wellington. The large rock, in the distance on your left as you approach Wellington's Monument, is Eagle Stone (said to resemble an eagle's head from a certain angle). It is a weathered block of gritstone, once a test of manhood for young men living in nearby villages. They had to climb the rock before they were allowed to marry.**

33. Go through gate and continue down. Eventually, as track becomes road, continue down past houses

34. As road (**Bar Road**) meets another (**Eaton Hill**), turn ***left*** and follow road down. Cross main road and walk to car park opposite

*Church Lane, Baslow*